31/54
91

WORKING WIVES/
WORKING HUSBANDS

Published in cooperation with (**ncfr**) National Council on Family Relations

Series Editor: **Maximiliane Szinovacz**

Books appearing in New Perspectives on Family are either single- or multiple-authored volumes or concisely edited books of original articles on focused topics within the broad field of marriage and family. Books can be reports of significant research, innovations in methodology, treatises on family theory, or syntheses of current knowledge in a subfield of the discipline. Each volume meets the highest academic standards and makes a substantial contribution to our knowledge of marriage and family.

SINGLES: Myths and Realities, *Leonard Cargan and Matthew Melko*

THE CHILDBEARING DECISION: Fertility Attitudes and Behavior, *Greer Litton Fox, ed.*

AT HOME AND AT WORK: The Family's Allocation of Labor, *Michael Geerken and Walter R. Gove*

PREVENTION IN FAMILY SERVICES: Approaches to Family Wellness, *David R. Mace, ed.*

Other volumes currently available from Sage and sponsored by NCFR:

ROLE STRUCTURE AND ANALYSIS OF THE FAMILY, *F. Ivan Nye*

CONFLICT AND POWER IN MARRIAGE: Expecting the First Child, *Ralph LaRossa*

THE AMERICAN FAMILY: A Demographic History, *Rudy Ray Seward*

THE SOCIAL WORLD OF OLD WOMEN: Management of Self-Identity, *Sarah H. Matthews*

ASSESSING MARRIAGE: New Behavioral Approaches, *Erik E. Filsinger and Robert A. Lewis, eds.*

SEX AND PREGNANCY IN ADOLESCENCE *Melvin Zelnik, John F. Kantner, and Kathleen Ford*

WORKING WIVES/ WORKING HUSBANDS

Joseph H. Pleck

Published in cooperation with
the National Council on Family Relations

SAGE PUBLICATIONS
Beverly Hills   London   New Delhi

For information address:

SAGE Publications, Inc.
275 South Beverly Drive
Beverly Hills, California 90212

SAGE Publications India Pvt. Ltd.
M-32 Market
Greater Kailash I
New Delhi 110 048 India

SAGE Publications Ltd
28 Banner Street
London EC1Y 8QE
England

Printed in the United States of America

Library of Congress Cataloging in Publication Data

Pleck, Joseph H.
  Working wives, working husbands.

  "National Council on Family Relations."
  Bibliography: p.
  1. Married people—Employment—Social aspects—
United States. 2. Sexual division of labor—United
States. 3. Sex role—United States. 4. Time manage-
ment—United States. 5. Family life surveys—United
States. I. National Council on Family Relations.
II. Title.
HQ536.P59 1985   306.8'7   85-11974
ISBN 0-8039-2489-5
ISBN 0-8039-2490-9 (pbk.)

FIRST PRINTING

Contents

Series Editor's Foreword

As researchers have come to recognize the increasing significance of the connections between paid work and housework, they have become correspondingly struck by how complicated and controversial the issue is. In this fascinating study, Joseph Pleck contributes to our understanding of the issue, but also shows us how incredibly complex it continues to be, and how much more research in the area needs to be done.

Pleck argues that an appropriate way to approach the entire matter is through what he calls "role overload theory." Using data from two national studies of how husbands and wives allocate time to housework, he attempts to determine the relative degree of "overload" experienced by working wives. His conclusion is that in the main while overload remains, it is declining because "men's time in the family is increasing while women's is decreasing." He provides some explanations for that conclusion and then goes on to show that over time not only have husbands of working wives increased their domestic involvements, so have husbands whose wives do *not* work. To account for that similarity he maintains that we are experiencing "a value shift in our culture towards greater family involvement by husbands."

Not that the millennium is upon us. He also argues that many men continue *not* to want to participate in housework to the degree that women do. He presents a number of possible reasons for that assertion, as well as a series of research questions for future investigations.

Pleck's study comes at an opportune time in the broader study of changes in family owing to women's employment. Scholars have disagreed regarding the degree of change that has actually occurred. But he shows us that within this realm there have indeed been some significant alterations. However, there is a great deal of continuity as well, and it is the task of subsequent investigators to probe the issue further examining among other matters, for example, the sorts of decision-making processes occurring in many U.S. families that allow the kinds of inequalities to be maintained that Pleck documents.

—John Scanzoni

Acknowledgments

Primary support for the research reported here was provided by the National Institute of Mental Health (MH 32620) and the National Science Foundation (SOC 7825695). Additional support for the initial and final phases of the research was provided by the National Institute of Mental Health (MH 29143) and by Time, Inc.

The data utilized in this research from the 1975–76 Study of Time Use in Social and Economic Accounts were made available by the Inter-University Consortium for Political and Social Research. These data were originally collected by F. Thomas Juster, Greg J. Duncan, John P. Robinson, and Frank P. Stafford, supported by the National Science Foundation and the U.S. Department of Health, Education, and Welfare. The data utilized in this research from the 1977 Quality of Employment Survey were originally collected by Robert P. Quinn, Stanley E. Seashore, Graham L. Staines, and Joseph H. Pleck, supported by the U.S. Department of Labor. Neither the original collectors of the data (except the present author), the funding agencies, the Consortium, nor the Wellesley College Center for Research on Women bear any responsibility for the analyses or interpretations presented here.

I wish to thank especially Michael Rustad for his conscientious and dedicated execution of the analysis of two complicated and difficult data sets. I also want to thank Linda Lang, Rebecca Fisher, Graham Staines, Laura Lein, Marguerite Rupp and Kathie DeMarco for their help in the conduct of this project. Phyllis Moen, Jeylan Mortimer, Jane Hood, and John Scanzoni commented on part or all of previous versions of this manuscript.

Earlier forms of material in Chapters 2 and 6 appeared in Pleck and Lang (1978) and Pleck and Rustad (1980a). The final report on the project on which this monograph is based appeared as Pleck (1982).

1

Wives' Employment and the Division of Family Work

Today's high rates of paid employment among women, and especially among wives, are well known. As this is written in mid-1984, women's labor force participation rate is 54 percent, compared to men's 78.4 percent (Bureau of Labor Statistics, 1984). Data for 1981 make possible more detailed breakdowns. In 1981, 51.8 percent of all women over the age of 16, and 50.3 percent of all wives with husbands present were in the labor force. Further, 55.7 percent of married women with children under the age of 18, and 47.8 percent of those with children under six years of age, were employed (Hayghe, 1982). Another important statistic is the proportion of all husband-wife couples in which both husband and wife are employed, compared to those in which the husband is the sole breadwinner. In 1981, 51.8 percent were two-earner couples, while the husband was the sole earner in only 23.6 percent (derived from Hayghe, 1982). (These two percentages do not add to 100 due to the relatively large number of couples in which neither spouse is in the labor force, and various other combinations, e.g., wife only, husband and someone besides the wife, etc.) Clearly, in American families in which both husband and wife are present, the dual-earner family is now the emerging majority.

It has been widely observed that these high rates of women's and especially wives' employment are having profound effects on the family and, more generally, on American society. In *The Subtle Revolution: Women at Work*, Smith (1979: 2) notes that "as more women work outside the home, the fight for equal treatment in the job market and equal responsibilities for unpaid domestic work has intensified. Indeed, female-male relationships in every aspect of society are being questioned and changing."

Less obvious, perhaps, than these effects is the impact of wives' employment on the way that family researchers and theorists have conceptualized the family. The study of couples in which both the husband and wife are employed has questioned old theoretical assumptions about the dynamics of husband-wife relationships, and brought to light issues needing empirical study that were formerly overlooked or taken for granted. The field of family research is, in many respects, still only beginning to respond to the profound challenge which wives' employment and the two-earner family poses to its traditional theoretical perspectives.

RESOURCE THEORY

One particular disparity between prevailing theories about the family and the new data arising from two-earner couples starting in the 1960s was the underlying stimulus for the research described in this book. This discrepancy concerned a topic that prior to this time had excited little interest in family research: husbands' and wives' performance of family work (i.e., housework and childcare). Before the 1970s, the division of family work between husbands and wives had been relatively neglected in the family field, and was becoming even more so. For example, in a 1962 text, Bernard deleted the material on housework and the housewife that had appeared in the 1949 edition (Glazer, 1976: 905n).

In contrast to topics like marital adjustment and marital power, which had been intensively studied since the 1930s, the division of labor became well-established as a research topic only in 1960, with the publication of Blood and Wolfe's highly influential study, *Husbands and Wives* (1960). This study developed an index of the division of housework between husband and wife which became the standard measure used in family research thereafter, used to demonstrate how the division of labor varies in relation to both socioeconomic variables and husbands' and wives' relative employment. Blood and Wolfe's classic study reported that in couples in which the wife is employed, husbands did more.

To explain this finding, as well as other results, Blood and Wolfe (1960: 73–74) proposed what has since become known as "resource theory":

> A few tasks, such as repairing or bookkeeping, require skills which may not be distributed equally in the family nor easily learned. Hence they are best performed by whoever has the technical know-how. Some tasks, such as lawn-mowing and snow-shovelling require muscular strength in which husbands usually surpass their wives. But most household tasks are humdrum and menial in nature; the chief resource required is time. Usually the person with the most time is the wife — provided she isn't working outside the home. If she does work, the husband incurs a moral obligation to help her out in what would otherwise be her exclusive task areas. And help her he does . . . The same bio-social reasons which shaped the traditional family still supply differential resources which men and women bring to marriage. But where resources differ from man to man or woman to woman, the modern family adjusts its division of labor accordingly.

To further support resource theory, Blood and Wolfe also performed a limited test of an alternative hypothesis: the division of household labor is determined by traditional family ideology. They tested this alternative hypothesis through comparison of the rural and urban families, and the Catholic and non-Catholic families within their sample, on the assumption that rural and Catholic families were more likely to hold traditional views of family roles. The researchers found hardly any differences between these groups in their division of household work. Thus, they concluded, husbands' relatively low contribution to family work did not derive from traditional ideology, but rather was a rational response to the fact that husbands have fewer resources, particularly time, with which to perform these tasks.

Blood and Wolfe's resource theory complemented two other theoretical notions that have been dominant in family studies: exchange theory, and the concept of role differentiation. Family researchers borrowed "exchange theory" from social psychology. In Scanzoni's (1970) particularly influential statement, husbands in effect exchange their successful performance of the family breadwinner role for their wives' provision of love, companionship, and household services. In this theory, each partner's contribution to the mutual exchange places an obligation on the other partner to provide his or her reciprocal contribution. Scanzoni's application of exchange theory to the family does not, in principle, imply that marital exchange always does or should take the form it does in traditional marriages in which only the husband is employed. Nonetheless, exchange theory was widely used as though it did.

In Parsons and Bales' (1955) classic formulation of role differentiation, the male's role is "instrumental", responsible for the family's relationships with the outside world, primarily through his job. The female's role is "expressive", and entails responsibility for dealing with the family's internal needs. Parsons and Bales believed that this kind of role differentiation is a universal feature of not just the family, but of all social groups. Thus, husbands were seen as doing relatively little family work as part of a larger pattern of sex role differentiation in which men specialize in the family breadwinner role while wives monopolize the housework and childcare inside the family. Blood and Wolfe (1960: 48) echoed this perspective when they wrote: "To a considerable extent, the idea of shared work is incompatible with the most efficient division of labor. Much of the progress of our modern economy rests upon the increasing specialization of its division of labor."

Resource theory was also joined by new economic models of family behavior, often referred to as the "new home economics" (Becker, 1976; Berk, 1980). These theories saw wives' time in housework and childcare as one component of a family strategy to maximize economic "utility", in the context of wives' and husbands' wages rates and productivity, in the paid labor market and the home market. As Glazer (1976: 907) expressed it, beginning with the Blood and Wolfe study, "the main theoretical perspective used to explain the division of labor — the wife's responsibility for 'feminine tasks' and the husbands' responsibility for 'masculine tasks' — is an assumed 'rational imperative' (based, of course, on the biological difference between the sexes)."

Thus, well into the 1970s, the dominant theoretical view in the family field of the division of labor between husbands and wives was a traditional perspective based on resource theory, but drawing as well on exchange theory and the concept of role differentiation, and complemented by economic theories of time allocation. This resource perspective held, in essence, that husbands' typically low level of family work was the result of their job role, not sex role ideology.

CONTRADICTORY DATA AND THE FEMINIST CRITIQUE

Data from large-scale surveys of time use conducted in the 1960s and early 1970s (but which did not become widely known to family researchers until the mid-1970s) entirely contradicted this traditional theoretical perspective as it applied to dual-earner couples. As described in more detail in Chapter 2, these time use studies consistently indicated that husbands of employed wives did *not* perform more housework and childcare than did husbands of full-time homemakers. As a result, employed wives' *total* work load (paid work plus housework and childcare) was considerably higher than their husbands', even though employed wives reduced their housework and childcare compared to housewives. The data indicated that employed wives experienced "role overload" (as this phenomenon came to be known) compared to their husbands, by a margin of 1.3 to 2.4 hours per day in the various available studies.

In light of these data, it became intellectually untenable to view the husband's limited family role as the result of an equitable exchange between husband and wife based on their having different resources. The traditional resource theory may have fit the data from the declining minority of families in which the husband is the sole breadwinner. But this traditional perspective breaks down when applied to the emerging majority of two-earner families.

It took some time for these time use research data to become known and accepted in the family field. I recall numerous exchanges with colleagues in the mid- and late 1970s who insisted that these results simply could not be true. How could husbands not increase their housework and childcare when their wives worked? Besides, they asked, hadn't Blood and Wolfe shown that husbands did? Only gradually and over time did these time use data contradicting Blood and Wolfe become recognized.

A major reason for the ultimate acceptance of the time use

results was their compatibility with the feminist critique of the family division of labor, one of the three principal critiques which contemporary feminism has made of the family, beginning in the 1970s. It is perhaps not widely recognized to what extent feminism is a theory of the family — more specifically, a theory of family inequality. This theoretical effort has taken a variety of forms in different intellectual disciplines — sociology, political science, history, ethics, psychology, economics, philosophy, and even others. Many different modes of analysis, let alone specific hypotheses, are apparent in this literature. Nonetheless, in nearly all of these theoretical efforts, women's roles as wife and mother are seen as a paradigm for women's subordination to men.

The precise nature of this subordination, however, has been formulated in at least three different ways. Some feminist writers and activists see men's physical violence and abuse of their wives as the central reality of the husband-wife relationship — an expression of men's maintenance of power over women through brute violence. Others view marital rape, supported by laws still extant in many states that specifically exempt husbands from prosecution for rape, as the epitome of the spousal relationship. Finally, yet others have identified the principal aspect of wives' oppression to be their provision of domestic service to men and to men's children. Violence, sexual domination, and domestic exploitation have thus been three clear but independent themes in the recent feminist critique of the family.

The third theme, family division of labor as exploitation of women, has itself been developed in a variety of ways. Pat Mainardi's (1970) well-known and pointedly titled essay, "The politics of housework", argued that housework inequality is a form of exploitation experienced by women in relationships with men. Wrote Mainardi (1970: 447–448):

> We women have been brainwashed . . . Probably too many years of seeing television women in ecstasy over their shiny waxed floors or breaking down over their dirty shirt collars. Men have no such conditioning. They recognize the essential fact of housework from the beginning. Which is that it stinks . . . All of us have to do these things, or get someone else to do them for us. The longer my husband contemplated these chores, the more repulsed he became, and so proceeded the change from the normally sweet considerate

Dr. Jekyll into the crafty Mr. Hyde who would stop at nothing to avoid the horrors of — *housework*. As he felt himself backed into a corner laden with dirty dishes, brooms, mops, and reeking garbage, his front teeth grew longer and pointier, his fingernails haggled, and his eyes grew wild. Housework trivial? Not on your life! Just try to share the burden.

This article was included in the early landmark collection *Sisterhood Is Powerful* (Morgan, 1970); Jessie Bernard quoted it at length in *The Future of Marriage* (1972), and other feminist scholars continue to cite and discuss it (e.g. Hartmann, 1981; Pogrebin, 1983). It is now included in collections of classic documents in American family history (Scott and Wishy, 1982).

Another early critical indictment of the traditional male family role, more widely known among academic feminists, was Polatnick's (1973–74) "Why men don't rear children: A power analysis." In contrast to Mainardi, Polatnick focussed on childcare, asserting that men burden women with housework and especially childcare responsibility as a deliberate strategy to maintain power over women themselves. In Polatnick's (1973–74: 79) words:

Whatever the "intrinsic desirability" of rearing children, the conditions of the job as it's now constituted — no salary, low status, long hours, domestic isolation — mark it as a job for women only. Men, as the superordinate group, don't want child-rearing responsibility, so they assign it to women. Women's functioning as child-rearers reinforces, in turn, their subordinate position.

Polatnick further argues that men's low participation in childcare is, in effect, a strategy men use to restrict women's ability to compete with them in the labor market.

Where outright forbidding of the wife to work is no longer effective, the continued allocation of child-rearing responsibility to the women accomplishes the same end: assuring male domination of the occupational world . . . The desire to limit females' occupational activities, and the desire to have children without limiting their own occupational activities . . . contribute to a male interest in defining child-rearing as exclusively woman's domain. (Polatnick, 1973–74: 64)

These early analyses of domestic exploitation developed in three distinct ways. One major line of analysis concerned the problems and issues of the full-time housewife (Gavron, 1966; Oakley, 1974; Andre, 1981). Simone de Beauvoir (quoted in Pogrebin, 1983: 148) wrote: "Few tasks are more like the torture of Sisyphus than housework with its endless repetition: the clean becomes soiled, the soiled is made clean, over and over, day after day. The housewife wears herself out marking time: she makes nothing, she simply perpetuates the present." These analyses focus on the low social valuation of housewives' role and the unstimulating nature of their actual work. Some analysts emphasize the negative aspects of the housewife role itself, while others interpret the problems of the role more in terms of the woman not having the financial, social, and emotional benefits that derive from employment (e.g., Gove, 1972; Bernard, 1972).

Another line of thought in the feminist critique of the division of labor is formulated within a Marxist framework (Glazer, 1976; Eisenstein, 1979). Arguments in this perspective view women as laborers exploited by men, in highly privatized work in the last remaining unrationalized sector of the economy. In addition to simple domestic service, women's child-bearing and child-rearing are also interpreted as the production of new workers. Hartmann (1981: 385, 386) refers to "the patriarchal benefits reaped in housework", arguing that "women of all classes are subject to patriarchal power in that they perform household labor for men." It is interesting to note that the primary way that Marxism has been integrated with the feminist critique of the family concerns family work, and not domestic violence or marital rape. The domestic division of labor and child-bearing are the aspects of the feminist critique of the family which Marxist theoretical apparatus can most easily be applied to.

The third and most recent line of argument about domestic exploitation, concerning "role overload", initially grew out of the Marxist analysis but gradually became independent of it. Whereas the two earlier arguments either focussed on the housewife or did not differentiate between housewives and employed wives, this argument focusses only on the latter. As documented by the time use studies cited at the outset of this section, the total work load (paid work and family work combined) of employed wives exceeds their husbands by a considerable margin.

The role overload argument was most explicitly formulated by Meissner et al. (1975) in "No exit for wives: Sexual division of labor and the cumulation of household demands." This time use study of 340 couples in Vancouver, B.C., was one of the three classic time use studies documenting the husband-wife differential in total work. In the study, Meissner et al. (1975: 437) postulated a "contradiction between economic change resulting in a greater demand for women's work, on the one hand, and the stability of sexist conventions in the allocation of work, on the other." Meissner et al. (1975: 426–427) predicted and found in the study that:

> increases in the paid working hours of husband or wife will increase the wife's workload . . . while men's workload will be unaffected by their wives' working time . . . As demands increase, the combined over-all workload of the couple increases, but the husband's workload remains stable, and his share in the workload, as well as in the increase, declines . . . The demands resulting from his wife's paid work will have little effect on the husband's total workload or his contribution to housework.

The construct of role overload was elaborated in a variety of ways. In English and other European feminist writings, employed wives' role overload was discussed under the term "the double day" (Malos, 1980). Vickery (1979: 197), in the influential Urban Institute volume *The Subtle Revolution*, observed that "The time-budget studies from the late 1960s raised the question of how long a full-time working wife would be willing to work seventy-one hours each week while her husband works fifty-five hours. Although such an unequal distribution of work might be expected during the period when a wife's work role is changing, wives cannot be expected to work such long hours indefinitely." According to Hartmann (1981: 383), "the rather small, selective, and unresponsive contribution of the husband to housework raises the suspicion that the husband may be a net drain on the family's resources of working time — that is, husbands may require more housework than they contribute. Indeed, this hypothesis is suggested by my materialist definition of patriarchy, in which men benefit directly from women's labor power." Hartmann (1981: 390) further argued that as a result of their overload, "women are resisting doing housework and rearing children, at least as many children."

The housework issue also surfaced among those concerned with men's changing roles. Farrell's *The Liberated Man* (1974), probably the most widely read book on "men's liberation", criticized men for doing so little housework and childcare, arguing it had negative effects on women and children, as well as on men themselves. Farrell noted that in his observation, housework was the issue that "liberated" men most avoided, even more than homosexuality and impotence (see also Glazer, 1976: 905). Succinctly tying together these arguments, Pogrebin (1983: 144) asserted that "a refusal to housework signals feminist rebellion for women, and resistance to 'women's liberation' among men."

Alva Myrdal (1967) put role overload in a perspective that further emphasized the interrelationship between role overload and change in male roles. With Viola Klein, Myrdal (1956) had earlier introduced the phrase "women's two roles" to describe how contemporary women have added a second role, in paid employment, to their traditional role in the family. In a 1967 article, she observed that women's having two roles cannot work over the long run unless men hold two roles as well — adding a greatly enlarged family role to their traditional role in paid employment.

Myrdal's argument implies that increased family participation is the single most important manifestation of change in the male role, just as increased labor force involvement is the most significant change in women's role. Other feminist analyses, however, see little evidence or hope for this change. According to Schram (1984: 43), for example:

> while the rhetoric for the all-involved "new father" is in place, behavior does not reflect the rhetoric . . . Instead of seeing husbands functioning as co-parents, we have witnessed a continuing relatively low level of paternal involvement, and a concomitant increase in the asymmetrical division of labor characterized by mothers working a double day.

THE ROLE OVERLOAD HYPOTHESIS

Thus, the division of family labor, once a relatively minor and low priority topic in family research, was now located at the center of the contemporary debate about sex roles and the family. Under the impetus of the feminist critique, the results of time use studies greatly stimulated family researchers' interest in husbands' responsiveness to their wives' employment and on employed wives' role overload. Previous theory and research came under detailed attack.

For example, Glazer (1976: 907) criticized the division of labor perspective (and even the construct of division of labor itself) as a "prefeminist or even antifeminist conception", limited by its "implicit sexism." As Vanek (1980: 276) summarized the critique of the traditional perspective:

> What unites these approaches [resource theory and the new home economics] is the emphasis on economic or pragmatic concerns and the neglect of the norms and values which continue to distinguish the duties and responsibilities of the sexes. The economic model ignores completely the cultural factors affecting the allocation of work; and "resource theory" which assumes that equalitarian beliefs are replacing the traditional ideology of sex differences, minimizes the influence of culture.

But if the traditional resource theory of the family division of labor is no longer valid, a theoretical perspective to replace it needed development. The basic realization that the division of labor in two-earner couples is inequitable can be theoretically extended in a variety of possible ways. Researchers have begun to formulate and test new or revised theories about the division of family labor and its relationships to other family and sex role dynamics. One of the most noteworthy is Geerken and Gove's (1983) analysis, drawing on but significantly modifying the economic theory of time allocation contained in the new home economics (Becker, 1976; Berk, 1980), which concerns the consequences of the relative wage level and productivity of husbands and wives. In Geerken and Gove's theory, the family's work-housework allocation is its imperfect attempt to maximize "utility", broadly defined, considered in its economic *and* social environment, with the latter specifically including expectations about the appropriate sexual division of labor as perceived by family members.

Huber and Spitze (1983), in an equally ambitious effort, propose a theory of "sex stratification" in which the division of family work is a central element. Explicitly critiquing the "new home economics" on both conceptual and empirical grounds, their theory argues that women's degree of labor force participation is the major variable accounting for the division of labor, not the husband-wife wage ratio. Like Gove and Geerken, Huber and Spitze's conceptualization includes sex role ideology as a variable, but interprets it as a consequence of wives' labor force participation rather than as a source of the division of labor.

Numerous other studies have attempted to analyze the dynamics by which family roles are divided between spouses in two-earner couples. For example, drawing on theoretical analyses of family conflict and decision-making by LaRossa (1977), Scanzoni (1978), and Scanzoni and Szinovacz (1980), Hood (1983) distinguishes between role *sharing* (the actual division of roles) and role *bargaining* (the process that results in a division (or redivision) of family roles). In a qualitative study, Hood finds that spouses' psychological involvement in their roles and their degree of role overload affect how resources determine bargaining power, and how bargaining power is used to shape the division of labor. As another example, Lein (1979, 1983; Lein et al., 1974) examine how husbands and wives attribute meanings to their roles that affect the division of labor. For example, the higher wages and family health benefits usually provided by the husband's job make it seem fair that wives should do more housework and childcare, even if they spend as many hours in paid work as their husbands.

This book investigates a set of five specific propositions about the division of family work in two-earner couples which I term the "role overload hypothesis." I have not attempted to develop the role overload hypothesis as a formal theory deriving directly from past sociological and economic approaches. Rather, in formulating it, I have tried to identify some of the major theoretical and empirical assumptions which have become prevalent in feminist research and thought concerning the division of family labor since the acceptance of the time use studies of the 1960s and early 1970s. The role overload hypothesis is simply a systematic statement of the critical ideas about the family division of labor which feminism has contributed to family sociology and family studies.

Investigating these propositions does not advance a specific line of theory by, for example, contributing a new refinement to the microeconomic theory of time allocation in the family, or to the Marxist analysis. Nor does it contribute to a macrosocial theory of the evolution of gender roles in modern societies, such as Geerken and Gove's, or Huber and Spitze's. Nor, of course, do the lines of argument within this hypothesis exhaustively include every idea or analytical point about the traditional division of labor expressed in the current studies discussed above. Rather, I assert that these five propositions constitute the set of related, core assumptions about husbands' and wives' work and family roles evident in contemporary research. Formulating these arguments at the level I have, and considering them together as a group significantly contributes, I believe, to our understanding of current changes and issues in women's and men's roles in family and paid work.

The role overload hypothesis consists of five propositions:

1. The division of family work is inequitable, in that husbands do not do more housework and childcare when their wives are employed, and employed wives spend more time in the sum of their work and family roles than do their husbands.

2. Traditional sex role ideology is a major determinant of the division of family work.

3. Most wives want their husbands to do more family work.

4. Employed wives' role overload has negative consequences for their well-being.

5. Husbands are much more psychologically involved in their paid work role than in the family role.

As we have already seen for proposition 1, and will see for the others in later chapters, these arguments are well-established in contemporary analyses of the two-earner family. Propositions 2 and 5 are, in effect, assumptions about the sources of the inequitable allocation of family work in couples. Likewise, propositions 3 and 4 are arguments about the consequences of this inequitable allocation. In a strict sense, however, the different propositions in the role overload hypothesis on the division of labor are relatively independent of each other, both logically and empirically. Nonetheless, they are linked by the fact they have been widely assumed to be true, and all derive from a more general value position that contemporary family behavior remains strongly influenced by traditional patterns of sex roles, which lead to particularly negative consequences for women. In sum, the role overload hypothesis, as expressed in much current research and popular thinking, holds that the division of family work in contemporary two-earner couples, deriving from traditional sex role ideology and husbands' low psychological involvement in the family, is inequitable, a source of conscious dissatisfaction to wives, and injurious to their well-being.

This book reports research undertaken to systematically explore the different propositions in the role overload hypothesis, using data from two different surveys of national representative samples conducted in the late 1970s. My effort is not to prove or disprove these propositions, or the perspective underlying them. Rather, my objective is to contribute to the current analysis of sex roles by identifying some of the essential ideas within this analysis as it is currently formulated, subjecting them to empirical examination, and interpreting which ones continue to be useful and which others need to be modified or reformulated in the light of new evidence.

PLAN OF THE BOOK

Chapter 2 summarizes the basic findings on husbands' and wives' time use in past research, and introduces the two surveys and samples used in the study, describing in detail how they assess time use. The chapter analyzes the levels of husbands' and wives' time expenditure at the job and in the family in relation to wives' employment status and stage of the family life cycle. This chapter indicates how the inequitable patterns of the marital division of family work revealed in earlier data have remained the same — or changed — in more recent years.

Chapter 3 examines the impact of time in paid work, sex role attitudes and sex on husbands' and wives' time in family work. It seeks to determine how well sex role ideology accounts for men's low level of family work compared to women, as well as how sex role ideology interacts with sex and with time in paid work.

Chapter 4 investigates wives' desire for the husbands to do

more housework and childcare. The effects of wives' and husbands' levels of family work on wives' desires for greater husband participation are examined, in addition to the direct and moderating effects of sex role attitudes. Brief attention is also given to husbands' perceptions of whether their wives want them to do more.

Chapter 5 presents analyses of the effects of time in family work, paid work, and the two combined on three measures of adjustment in both wives and husbands: family adjustment, feelings of time pressure, and overall well-being. These analyses also make use of wives' desires for greater husband participation as variables moderating the impact of employed wives' patterns of time use on their adjustment.

Chapter 6 examines husbands' and wives' psychological involvement in paid work and family roles, testing the common idea that husbands' primary psychological involvement is in their job, not their family life. This notion is explored both through husbands' direct self-reports about their psychological involvement and satisfaction in the two roles, as well as through analysis of the impact of satisfaction in the two domains on individuals' well-being.

Finally, Chapter 7 offers an interpretation of what the issues about the division of family work between husbands and wives really are today, in light of the preceding analyses.

2

Basic Patterns of Family
Work and Paid Work

Researchers on work and occupations have traditionally paid considerable attention to the amount and scheduling of the time that workers spend at their jobs. By contrast, the field of family studies has given much less emphasis to husbands' and wives' time investment in their family roles, especially housework and childcare (family work). Instead, family research has predominantly focussed on topics such as how individuals choose their mates, marital power and decision-making, and marital adjustment.

When researchers have investigated the family work that spouses perform, they have typically conceptualized it in terms of how husbands and wives divide up housework and childcare between themselves, rather than in terms of how much and what kinds of family work each actually does. This conceptualization leads to the use of "proportional" measures of family work. The most important and widely used example is the eight-item division of labor index developed by Blood and Wolfe (1960) in *Husbands and Wives*, one of the most influential books in the history of family research. Respondents (usually wives) were asked who performed each of a list of tasks. In this measure, respondents rate eight different family tasks as being performed entirely by the husband; by the husband more than the wife; by the husband and wife equally; by the wife more than the husband; or, by the wife entirely.

This kind of measure has the advantage that it is relatively easy for individuals to respond to. Respondents seem to have little trouble estimating the relative contribution they and their spouses make to various tasks. The major drawback of proportional measures is that they do not provide data on how much family work either the husband or wife does individually.

That is, we could not use the results of studies employing proportional measures to describe the actual amount (as opposed to the proportion) of housework and childcare husbands typically do. Further, using this kind of measure to examine variations in the amount of family work performed can also be misleading. For example, if this measure indicates that the husband performs a higher proportion of the housework in couple A than couple B, we cannot really say whether husband A spends more time in family work than does husband B. This may be so, but it could also simply be that *wife A* performs *less* family work than does wife B. Thus, we cannot tell whether differences in scores on proportional measures of family work reflect differences in husbands' behavior, wives' behavior, or some combination of both.

Until the present, proportional measures, especially Blood and Wolfe's, have dominated research on couples' performance of housework and childcare. This research did not seem to produce startling or intriguing results. Some variations in the division of labor appeared to be associated with family life cycle stage and with various measures of social class. When wives were employed, husbands, as expected, did more in the family, as assessed by these measures. Altogether, the division of labor stimulated little interest, and was eclipsed by other issues. For example, major collections of articles reviewing key areas in family research such as the *Journal of Marriage and Family*'s "Decade Reviews" in 1970 and 1980 omitted this topic entirely. Bahr's (1974) review of research on the effects of wives' employment on marital power and division of labor devotes 15 pages to the former, but only four pages to the latter, primarily Blood and Wolfe's (1960) study and several others replicating it.

TIME USE: A NEW APPROACH

Using methods originally developed by home economists in the 1920s, a few researchers in the late 1960s began studying the amount of time that husbands and wives spend in family tasks. In the most elaborate kind of time use measure, "time diary" or "time budget" methodology, respondents record all their activities for a particular day on a 24-hour diary form. These activities are then coded, and summary measures for time spent in housework and childcare can be derived. A less elaborate time use method, "respondent summary estimates", asks respondents to make estimates of the total amount of time they spend in housework or childcare tasks for given periods like "yesterday", "the average day", or "last week".

Like proportional measures, time use measures have both advantages and limitations. Their advantage is that they yield separate figures for each spouse's family work in absolute terms, and in an easily understood unit of measurement, time. However, time diaries are expensive and difficult to collect. Further, exact data about an individual day may not be very useful as an indicator of the individual's typical patterns of time use, particularly if the researcher is interested in analyzing the correlates of variation in time use within a sample rather than in estimating population averages. Asking respondents to estimate how they spend time in various categories on the average day might get around this problem, but respondents frequently have difficulty making such estimates, and these estimates may be inaccurate.

Time use studies produced results that, for the first time, described how much husbands and wives actually did in absolute terms. These studies cast an entirely different perspective on the situation of employed wives. Time use data made it possible to study two issues in dual-earner families that proportional division of labor measures do not: Do husbands do more in the family in absolute terms when their wives are employed, and how does the total work load of employed wives and their husbands (that is, the sum of their time at their separate jobs and in housework and childcare) compare to each other?

Wives' employment status is only one of many possible determinants of husbands' level of family work. Nonetheless, the effect of wives' employment on husbands' housework and childcare is worth singling out for special attention. The presence or absence of an increase in husbands' family work when their wives are employed is important for our understanding of the reasons for husbands' typically low level of family work, and of the normative division of paid work and family work roles by husbands and wives. According to the conventional wisdom, husbands do relatively little in the family because they are employed, whereas their wives are not; the asymmetry of family work roles and the asymmetry of paid work roles complement each other. If this is so, husbands ought to take over more family work when their wives take over some of the economic breadwinning.

The question of the comparative work loads of husbands and wives in two-earner families is also an important one. When wives work outside the home, their level of family work presumably goes down. But depending on how much it goes down — and whether and how their husbands' time at their jobs and/or in the families changes — employed wives may have higher total work loads than their husbands. If so, employed wives, compared to their spouses, experience "role overload."

Table 2.1 summarizes findings from three major time use studies in the mid-1960s and early 1970s: Walker and Woods'

TABLE 2.1 Employed Husbands' and Wives' Time Use (Hours/Day) in Paid Work, Family Work, and All Work: Previous Studies

Study	*Time Use Category*	*Employed Husbands*		*Wives*	
		Wife Employed	*Wife Not Employed*	*Employed*	*Not Employed*
Walker &	Family Work	1.6	1.6	4.8	8.1
Woods (1976)[a]	Paid Work	6.3	7.8	5.3	.5[b]
	All Work	7.9	9.4	10.1	8.6
Robinson	Family work	1.1	1.0	4.0	7.6
(1977a)[c]	Paid Work	5.8	6.5	5.3	0
	All Work	6.9	7.5	9.3	7.6
Meissner	Family Work	.6	.6	2.3	4.6
et al.	Paid Work	7.1	7.7	6.5	1.9[b]
(1975)[d]	All Work	7.7	8.3	9.0	6.5

a. Data collected 1967–68; "employed wives" here are wives with 30 or more hours per week of paid work; Walker and Woods (Table 3.17) also report data for 1–14 hours, 15–19 hours, and 15–29 hours of wives paid employment.
b. Includes unpaid volunteer work.
c. Data collected 1965–66; estimated from Robinson (1977a, Tables 3.6–8; Robinson et al., 1977, Tables 1–2); Robinson's data not presented in entirely consistent form; estimates represent author's best judgment.
d. Data collected 1971; figures estimated from graphs.

(1976) survey of 1,296 wives in upstate New York in 1967–68; Robinson's (1977a) survey of 1,244 adults aged 18–65 from a national representative sample of non-farm households in which at least one person was employed ten or more hours a week, supplemented by 788 residents of Jackson, Michigan, meeting the same criteria, interviewed in 1965–66; and Meissner et al.'s (1975) survey of 221 households in Vancouver, B.C., in 1971. It should be noted that the figures in this summary for paid work hours appear low because they are expressed in hours per day averaged across both working *and* non-working days.

These three studies consistently show that husbands do not participate more in housework and childcare when their wives are employed. This seemingly contradicts Blood and Wolfe's (1960) conclusion that when wives hold jobs, "The husband feels obliged to help out more at home and takes over an appreciably larger share of the housework" (p. 63). However, this contradiction is only an apparent one, since Blood and Wolfe's measure assessed husbands' and wives' relative proportions of the total housework performed by the couple, not either spouse's participation in absolute terms. Time use studies indeed demonstrate that wife-employed husbands do a higher proportion of the family work, but only because wives' absolute level goes down, not because husbands' goes up. A prior study by Blood and Hamblin (1958), in fact, had estimated husbands' proportional shift as from 15 percent to 25 percent, figures exactly consistent with Walker and Woods' (1976) time use data.

The finding that when wives are employed, husbands do not do more in the family, has stirred considerable controversy. For example, Hoffman (1977, p. 653) holds, though with some qualifications, that in analyses in Robinson (1977a) and Walker and Woods (1976) in families with children, and which control for the number of children, husbands of employed wives do contribute more family work. Actually, though Robinson conducted no analysis restricted to families with children, in his analysis controlling for the number of children, husbands of employed wives performed six minutes more per day of housework, and one minute less per day of primary childcare. The former measure had a mean of 52 and a pooled standard deviation of 81 for the two groups of husbands. On a peripheral measure, child "contact" (time in all activities in which a child is present, which includes considerable leisure time as well as time in which the wife is present), husbands of employed wives spent an average of 19 minutes more per day, as against a mean of 115 and a pooled standard deviation of 153. Whether these data, taken together, show an increment in husbands' family work associated with wives' employment is a matter of judgment. Hoffman also cites Walker and Gauger's (1973) early report from the Walker and Woods (1976) study, in which comparisons between husbands of employed and nonemployed wives are made in 19 different subgroups according to number of children, age of youngest child, and wife's age. Among the 15 subgroups in which children are present, wife-employed husbands do more family work than sole-breadwinning husbands in 8, less in 6, and the same in 1. For both studies, Hoffman and I make quite different judgments about whether the pattern of results indicates an overall increase in husbands' family participation.

Ericksen, Yancey, and Ericksen (1979) reject my interpretation (first offered in Pleck, 1977) that the discrepancy between Blood and Wolfe's results and those of the time use studies is due to the difference between proportional and absolute measures. They state: "It is hard to imagine though that this could reconcile Vanek's estimate of three hours per week for husbands of women who work (and perform an average of 26 hours per week housework) with Blood and Wolfe's estimate that when the wife works, a large proportion of husbands do half the housework" (p. 304). Ericksen et al. misleadingly contrast the lowest estimate of wife-employed husbands' family work ever made in a time use study with a basic misunderstanding of what Blood and Wolfe actually found. The figure attributed to Vanek (1973, p. 153) is wives' estimate of their husbands' housework in Robinson's 1965–66 survey (p. 153); time diary data from the husbands themselves were not yet available for analysis, though Vanek noted preliminary analyses gave an average value of seven hours per week (p. 154), a figure revised drastically upward to 11.3 hours per week in Robinson's (1977a, p. 64) final monograph.

As quoted earlier, Blood and Wolfe state that the wife-employed husband "takes over an appreciably larger share of the housework," but nowhere indicate that husbands do half. Indeed, Blood's earlier study (Blood & Hamblin, 1958) gave an estimate of 25 percent for the two-earner husband's share.

The scoring of Blood and Wolfe's division of labor index may contribute to the confusion. They first describe (p. 49) deriving a "relative task participation" score from the index as the average response to the eight items on a five-point scale (one = husband always; five = wife always). In their discussion of the relationship between the marital division of labor and other variables such as wives' employment (pp. 60–62), however, they shift to another kind of summary score, "wife's mean task performance." Its exact calculation is nowhere discussed, but it appears to be the number of tasks (out of eight) which the wife reports she does more often than her husband, or always (i.e., the number of items with scores of four and five on the original measure). The average score on this measure in couples in which the husband is employed full-time and the wife is also employed is 3.4. This might give the impression that husbands do a little more than half. However, the eight items in the measure were deliberately chosen to include equal numbers of traditional male and female tasks (three of each, plus two neutral tasks). Thus this measure highly overrepresents husbands' task performance relative to husbands' and wives' actual time expenditure in family work. Performing half the tasks included in this measure can hardly be interpreted as showing that husbands do half the housework.

The second conclusion evident in Table 2.1 is that employed wives' total work load is higher than their husbands. Across the three studies, the extent of employed wives' relative role overload ranges from 1.3 to 2.4 hours per day. On this finding, there is no dispute.

The time use results to Table 2.1 have a major limitation, however. The data on which they are based were collected between 1965 and 1971. One of the present study's goals is to describe and analyze the patterns of work and family time use in two-earner as compared to one-earner families in more recent data. Have husbands' and wives' patterns of time use changed? Are husbands now more likely to increase their family work when their wives are employed? Are employed wives still overloaded compared to their husbands?

THE TWO SURVEYS AND THEIR
MEASURES OF TIME USE

To answer these questions (and the other research questions posed in Chapter 1), I turned to data from two national surveys conducted in the mid- and late 1970s: The 1975–76 Study of Time Use in Economic and Social Accounts (hereafter the Study of Time Use, or STU) and the 1977 Quality of Employment Survey (QES). These two surveys collected data about husbands' and wives' time use in quite different ways. (Measures of several other constructs from both surveys are used in the analyses in later chapters as they are needed.)

1975–76 Study of Time Use (STU)

The 1975–76 Study of Time Use was a replication and expansion of the 1965–66 National Time Diary Study conducted by Robinson (1977a) and reported in Table 2.1. It was carried out by the Institute for Social Research, University of Michigan, and interviewed a total of 2,406 persons. Of these, 1,519 were "primary respondents", a representative sample of individuals aged 18 and over drawn from a national probability sample of households, following usual ISR sampling procedures. An additional sample of 887 spouses of these primary respondents were also interviewed. The study's design called for every individual to complete a 24-hour time diary at four different times over the course of a year. Individuals were interviewed in person during the fall of 1976. They were then reinterviewed by telephone three times during 1976: in February, May, and September. For further information on sampling and other details of the 1975–76 STU, see Juster et al. (1978) and Juster and Stafford (in press). Retrospective time diaries were collected for the full 24-hour day preceding each of the four interviews. Starting at 12 midnight, respondents were asked to describe what they were doing and other questions concerning where they were (and for primary respondents, who was with them, and what else they were doing at the same time). For each activity, respondents were asked what time the activity stopped, which then became the starting time of the next activity. Respondents averaged somewhat over 20 acts per day in their diaries.

Each act was coded according to a modified form of the 96-category system used in Szalai (1972) and Robinson (1977a, 1977c). Time in these detailed categories was then aggregated into four categories of family work (basic and other housework, and basic and other childcare). Summary categories for paid work and sleep were also developed. Table 2.2 shows the detailed categories (identified by the name and code number used in Juster et al., 1978) contributing to each summary category. In later analyses, basic and other housework are also summed as all housework (likewise for childcare), housework and childcare are summed as all family work, and family work and paid work are summed as all or total work. More details on the coding categories and how they differ from those used in earlier studies are given in Pleck and Rustad (1980b).

Information from the time diaries collected in the 1975–76 STU was aggregated across the four waves of interviewing. The survey design called for collecting time diaries from each individual for one Saturday, one Sunday, and two week days. The order of week day and weekend days was balanced across the four interviews. For individuals from whom time diaries were successfully collected for both weekend days and at least one week day, the ISR research team calculated the amount of time spent in each category for a hypothetical "synthetic week." This was derived as the sum of the Saturday time, the Sunday time, and 2.5 times each week day time (if two week day diaries were collected) *or* 5.0 times the one week day time (if only one week day diary was collected). For about 13 percent of the individuals with time use calculated for the synthetic week, these estimates were based on three rather than four days.

The 1975–76 STU provides the most comprehensive set of data on time use ever collected for a sample of individuals. While all other time diary studies collect a diary for only a single day per respondent, this study collected diaries for four days. By combining data from these four diaries into the "synthetic week", we can analyze the levels and correlates of housework, childcare, and other activities with greater confidence that the time use figures for an individual reflect that person's typical pattern than if only a single diary were available.

TABLE 2.2 Components of Summary Time Use Categories: 1975–76 Study of
Time Use

Summary Category	Activities (with Code Numbers)[a]
Basic Housework	Meal preparation (10) Meal cleanup (11) Indoor cleaning (12) Outdoor cleaning (13) Laundry (14) Everyday shopping (30)
Other Housework	Gardening/pet care (17) Durable/house shopping (31) Government/financial services (34) Repair services (35) Other services (37) Service travel (39) Repairs, maintenance (16) Other household (19) Adult medical care (41) Adult other care (42)
Basic Childcare	Baby care (20) Child care (21) Medical care—kids (26)
Other Childcare	Helping/teaching (22) Reading/talking (23) Indoor playing (24) Outdoor playing (25) Babysitting/other (27) Travel-childcare (29)
Paid Work	Normal work (1) Unemployment acts (2) Second job (5) Before/after/other work (7) Coffee breaks (8) Travel to work (9)
Sleep	Night sleep (45) Naps, resting (46)

a. Activity names and code numbers as given in codebook (Juster et al., 1978).

At the same time, using these multiple-diary data to full advantage for the purposes of this study required excluding a considerable number of cases. The present analysis includes 249 employed husbands, 143 employed wives, and 155 nonemployed wives, all currently living with their spouses, from the STU. The total analysis sample was 547 cases, about only a quarter of cases originally interviewed. Approximately 25 percent of the cases were dropped because they were not currently married. Another quarter was omitted because it provided fewer than three time diaries during the four waves of interviewing, the minimum number of diaries needed to estimate their time use for the synthetic week, or had other anomalies in their time diaries.

The remaining quarter of the sample was excluded for two other reasons which are initially less obvious. First, the distinction between two-earner couples and couples in which only the husband is employed is central to all the analyses in this book. Actually, wives' and to a lesser extent husbands' employment status changes relatively frequently. Clearly, couples in which the husband is not consistently employed across the four interviews, or in which the wife is not consistently employed *or* consistently not employed, have to be dropped from the analysis. Nearly half of the married individuals who completed at least three time diaries were excluded because they were in a couple which did not meet these criteria. Finally, another smaller group of cases was eliminated because they were employed, but their time diaries indicated they worked at least partly on weekends and/or did not work on some week days. These patterns cause certain biases in the estimates of time use for the synthetic week. Pleck and Rustad (1980b) provide more information on this and other sampling issues.

Because the husbands and wives in the 1975–76 STU were married to each other, information was available for analysis on the time use of an individual's spouse. However, there was considerable missing data on spouses' time use, due to situations in which the spouse was interviewed but did not successfully complete the requisite number of diaries for the calculation of the synthetic week. ("Spouse" here refers simply to the partner of any individual interviewed in the survey, not to the distinction between "primary respondent" and "primary respondent's spouse" in the survey's sampling design.) Spouse's data is used in some analyses in this book, but is not used routinely.

1977 Quality of Employment Survey (QES)

Whereas the STU was designed and developed by other investigators, I was one of the four researchers at the Institute for Social Research who conducted the 1977 Quality of Employment Survey. The QES interviewed 1,515 persons aged 16 and over who were currently employed more than 20 hours per week. These individuals were drawn from a national probability sample of households, again following standard sampling procedures. Respondents were personally interviewed once during October–December 1977. The interview completion rate for respondents determined to be eligible in the sample was 72 percent. For further information on sampling and other details of the 1977 QES, see Quinn and Staines (1979).

The present analysis includes the 692 employed husbands and 220 employed wives with valid data on their family time use interviewed in the survey. The major respect in which this sample departs from national representativeness is its under-representation of individuals in two-earner couples. This logically resulted from the usual survey practice of selecting only one eligible respondent per household, combined with this survey's employment criterion. Since dual-earner couples by definition had at least two eligible respondents per household, members of these couples had about half the probability of entering the sample as individuals in couples in which only one spouse was employed.

It was not possible to administer time diaries in the QES. Instead, respondents were asked to estimate their time use in family and paid work. Housework was assessed by respondents' estimates, separately for workdays and nonworkdays, of how much time they spent on the average on "home chores — things like cooking, cleaning, repairs, shopping, yardwork, and keeping track of money and bills." "Home chores" was chosen as a term for household work which is more sex-neutral than "housework", which men might underreport due to its feminine connotations. Tasks exemplifying the term were selected to include both traditional masculine and feminine tasks, and to include tasks necessary for the functioning of the household conducted both inside and outside the home. To provide a measure of childcare, respondents with children under 17 in the household likewise estimated, separately for workdays and nonworkdays, the time they spent "taking care of or doing things with your child(ren)" if the youngest child was under ten, or the time they spent "doing things with your child(ren)" if the youngest was ten or over. For both housework and childcare measures, respondents were encouraged to respond in hours, fractions of hours, or minutes; all figures reported here are in hours. Following inspection of the distributions of the numerical estimates, nonnumerical responses such as "the whole day" were converted to values of eight hours for workdays and 16 hours for nonworkdays. Weekly estimates for home chores and childcare were derived by summing workday and nonworkday estimates, appropriately multiplied by the respondent's number of workdays or nonworkdays. Time in paid work was taken from respondents' self-reports of their weekly hours on their main job, excluding time taken for meals, but including time in second jobs, if any.

The use of the respondent summary estimate method in the 1977 QES has several consequences. Most obviously, respondents' estimates are more vulnerable to subjective distortion than are estimates taken from actual time diaries. Second, it should be noted that the childcare estimate in the 1977 QES includes a much broader range of activities than the most restricted childcare measure in the 1975–76 STU. Robinson (1977a) describes a broader "child contact" measure which can be derived from time diaries, including time in all activities in which a child is coded as present. Respondents' estimates of their childcare time in the 1977 QES is probably more comparable to the more extended "child contact" than the narrower "childcare" coded from time diaries. ("Child contact" data was not directly available in the 1975–76 STU dataset.)

Respondents in the 1977 QES were asked to estimate their spouses' time use in childcare (but not housework). These data were not used in this analysis, however, because of the high rate of "don't know" responses and other evidence of lack of validity, as well as the absence of a childcare measure needed to estimate all family work for spouses.

The 1975–76 STU and the 1977 QES clearly employed quite different methods to assess husbands' and wives' time use in the family. Using these two surveys together makes it possible to compare the results generated by these two methodologies.

FINDINGS ON FAMILY WORK
AND PAID WORK

Tables 2.3–4 display data from the 1975–76 STU and the 1977 QES on husbands' and wives' time in family work and paid work in one- and two-earner couples. Cell means are adjusted within sex for differences between subgroups in their distributions on parental status (three categories, as shown in Tables 2.5–8).[1] In summary, the results from each survey differ from those of earlier time use studies, but in different and inconsistent ways. In the 1975–76 STU, consistent with earlier studies, husbands show no appreciable increment in family work when their wives are employed. Further, there appears to be no difference in the proportions of housework and childcare in one- and two-earner husbands' family work. However, unlike earlier research, employed wives in this survey show only negligibly higher total work than their husbands (only 0.2 hours/day more).

By contrast, data from the 1977 QES differs from earlier research in suggesting that husbands do more family work. However, these data confirm earlier research in finding that employed wives have substantially greater work loads than their husbands (about 2.2 hours/day more).

The 1977 QES's respondent summary estimate procedure yields higher time use values than does the 1975–76 STU's time diary procedure. Housework estimates range from 9 to 28 percent higher than the diary figures in the subgroups that can be compared; respondents' estimates of their childcare are 317 to 650 percent higher, reflecting the broader definition of childcare in the QES. The figures for paid work are more similar in the two surveys, but the requirement that respondents in the QES (but not the STU) be employed 20 hours/week complicates this comparison.

TABLE 2.3 Employed Husbands' and Wives' Weekly Time Use (Hours/Day) in Family Work, Paid Work and All Work: 1975–76 Study of Time Use[a]

Time Use Category	Employed Husbands				Wives			
	All Husbands	Wife Employed	Wife Not Employed	Difference (WE−WNE)	All Wives	Wife Employed	Wife Not Employed	Difference (WE−WNE)
Housework	1.61	1.63	1.59	.04	4.52	3.37	5.60	−2.23***
Childcare	.24	.24	.25	−.01	.91	.64	1.16	−.52***
Family Work	1.85	1.87	1.83	.04	5.43	4.00	6.76	−2.76***
Paid Work[b]	6.96	6.89	7.04	−.15	2.44	4.95	.09	4.86***
All Work	8.81	8.76	8.87	−.11	7.87	8.96	6.84	2.12***
Basic Housework	.67	.69	.64	.05	3.55	2.71	4.33	−1.62***
Other Housework	.94	.94	.94	.00	.97	.66	1.27	−.61***
Basic Childcare	.10	.09	.10	−.01	.53	.36	.69	−.32***
Other Childcare	.14	.14	.14	.00	.38	.28	.47	−.19***
Sleep	7.96	7.95	7.97	.02	8.26	7.98	8.52	−.54***
N	249	129	120		298	143	155	

NOTE: Husbands and wives in the sample are married to each other, and are in couples in which the husband is employed. Rounding errors may cause slight discrepancies in sums.

a. Means for the subgroups according to wives' employment are adjusted within sex by MCA for differences in subgroup distributions on parental status, and the number of diary days reported to be "unusual". Unadjusted subgroup means are given in Tables 3.4 and 3.5.

b. Eight wives describing themselves as not employed reported time coded as paid employment in their diaries.

*** $p < .001$

TABLE 2.4 Employed Husbands' and Employed Wives' Weekly Time Use
(Hours/Day) in Family Work, Paid Work, and All Work by
Wives' Employment Status: 1977 Quality of Employment Survey

| Time Use Category | All Husbands | Employed Husbands | | | Employed Wives (6) |
		Wife Employed[a]	Wife Not Employed[a]	Difference (WE − WNE)	
Housework	1.83	1.98	1.73	.25*	4.30
Childcare	1.61	1.80	1.50	.30**	2.67
Family Work	3.52	3.87	3.32	.55**	6.97
Paid Work	6.76	6.54	6.89	−.34**	5.62
All Work	10.25	10.40	10.21	.20	12.59
N	692	257	435	—	220

NOTE: Husbands and wives in this sample are not married to each other. Rounding
errors may cause slight discrepancies in sums.
a. Means for the subgroups according to wives' employment status are adjusted by MCA
for differences in subgroup distributions on parental status. Unadjusted subgroup means
are given in Table 3.6.
* $p < .05$
** $p < .01$

Other Analyses in the 1975–76 STU

Because of the discrepancy between the present results on
employed wives' role overload in the 1975–76 STU and those of
previous time use research, several additional analyses (not
described in detail here) were conducted. The analysis in Table
2.3 was repeated with five categories of parental status
(distinguishing those with youngest children aged 6–12 and 13–
17, and those over and under age 45 among those with children),
and introducing number of children, education, and race as
additional covariates. The same comparisons were made with the
synthetic week data for those with no missing data on the
respondent's or spouse's employment status across the four
waves of interviewing; additionally restricting the definition of
employed respondents and spouses to those employed 35 or
more hours per week in Wave 1; and excluding certain categories
from paid work (coffee breaks, time at the workplace before and
after work) on which sex differences have been reported
(Stafford and Duncan, 1978). These comparisons all led to even
smaller estimates of the difference between employed wives' and
employed husbands' total work.

This comparison was also performed with the first wave data only, for those in the synthetic week sample (but not restricted to those with consistent employment statuses for themselves and their spouses across the four waves). In this comparison, estimates were derived for the subsamples of each marital group interviewed on a week day or a weekend day in Wave 1. These were converted into weekly estimates for each marital group by multiplying the former by five and the latter by two, and adding them together. This comparison estimated employed wives' total work to be about .5 hours per day more than that of husbands with employed wives.[2] This relative overload occurred entirely in the subsample of each marital group who were interviewed on a weekend day, with *N*'s of less than 50 for both employed husbands and employed wives. For the considerably larger week day subsamples of each group, employed wives performed *less* total work than did their husbands. Thus, the importance of the Wave 1 finding is not clear. In any case, even in the Wave 1 comparison, employed wives' role overload relative to their husbands is still small — only one-third the size of the smallest differential found in the earlier studies.

Tables 2.3 and 2.5–6 provide information on several other important points concerning marital time use in relation to wives' employment in the 1975–76 STU. These data include only a slight and non-significant increase of about .04 hours per day in husbands' family work when their wives are employed. This increase occurs primarily in husbands' basic housework. These husbands also show a non-significant decrease of about .15 hours a day in their paid work time. As a result of these two trends, husbands whose wives are employed spend about .11 hours less in total work per day than do sole-breadwinning husbands.

Analysis of husbands' time use controlling for parental status (Table 2.5) reveals one noteworthy variation from this general pattern. Fathers of preschool-aged children whose wives are employed spend about .37 *more* hours per day in paid work than fathers of similarly-aged children whose wives are not employed. These fathers in fact show the longest paid work day of any husband subgroup in the sample. That is, in this group, unlike both other parental status groups, there appears to be no trade-

TABLE 2.5 Employed Husbands' Time Use (Hours/Day) in Family Work, Paid Work, and All Work by Wives' Employment Status and Parental Status: 1975–76 Study of Time Use

Time Use Category	Youngest Child 0–5		Youngest Child 6–17		No Children in Household	
	WE	WNE	WE	WNE	WE	WNE
Housework	1.38	1.34	1.74	1.77	1.76	1.64
Childcare	.43	.44	.26	.29	.03[a]	.02[a]
Family Work	1.81	1.78	2.00	2.06	1.79	1.66
Paid Work	7.41	7.04	6.78	7.29	6.61	6.88
All Work	9.23	8.82	8.78	9.35	8.41	8.54
Basic Housework	.61	.59	.73	.52	.73	.82
Other Housework	.77	.74	1.01	1.25	1.03	.82
Basic Childcare	.25	.25	.04	.06	0.0	0.0
Other Childcare	.18	.19	.22	.23	.03[a]	.02[a]
Sleep	7.85	7.90	7.98	7.78	8.02	8.24
N	29	52	44	36	56	32

NOTE: All husbands in sample are employed. Rounding errors may cause slight discrepancies in sums.
WE = Wife employed.
WNE = Wife not employed.
a. Includes care to children outside the household.

off (i.e., a negative relationship) between husbands' paid work hours and wives' employment. Rather, in couples with preschool children, both are high. It may be that among many families in this group, family economic need relative to the husbands' earning power is so severe that both wives must take paid jobs *and* husbands must work unusually long hours.

Consistent with earlier research, employed wives show less time in family work than do non-employed wives — about 40 percent less in the present data. This decrease appears to be relatively equally distributed across all four subcategories of family work examined here. The decrease in the "other housework" subcategory, however, appears to be proportionately somewhat larger than in the other three subcategories.

When these effects for wives are examined within parental statuses (Table 2.6), the proportional decrement in the family work of employed wives compared to non-employed wives is proportionately greatest among couples with no children (about

TABLE 2.6 Wives' Weekly Time Use (Hours/Day) in Family Work, Paid Work, and All Work by Wives' Employment Status and Parental Status: 1975–76 Study of Time Use

Time Use Category	Youngest Child 0–5		Youngest Child 6–17		No Children in Household	
	WE	WNE	WE	WNE	WE	WNE
Housework	3.48	5.25	3.71	5.97	3.02	5.62
Childcare	1.20	2.16	.52	1.16	.11	.14[a]
Family Work	4.69	7.40	4.24	7.14	3.12	5.76
Paid Work	4.35	.05[b]	4.79	.05[b]	5.54	.06[b]
All Work	9.04	7.45	9.03	7.18	8.67	5.82
Basic Housework	2.88	4.41	2.98	4.59	2.28	3.98
Other Housework	.60	.83	.74	1.38	.73	1.64
Basic Childcare	.75	1.51	.22	.51	.02	.03[a]
Other Childcare	.46	.65	.30	.65	.09	.11[a]
Sleep	7.95	8.48	7.93	8.33	8.08	8.78
N	30	64	57	48	56	43

NOTE: All wives in the sample have employed husbands. Rounding errors may cause slight discrepancies in sums.
WE = Wife employed.
WNE = Wife not employed.
a. Includes care to children outside the household.
b. Eight wives describing themselves as not employed reported time coded as paid employment in their diaries.

45 percent) and least among couples with young children (about 37 percent). Interestingly, employment appears to cause the greatest decrement in family work among the group of wives doing the least family work to begin with, and least decrement among the group of wives doing the most.

Finally, non-employed wives show a markedly lower total work load than all other groups, i.e., than employed wives, and husbands of both employed and non-employed wives. In particular, they spend about two fewer hours per day in total work than do their husbands. As evident in Table 2.1, previous research suggests that total work load of non-employed wives is lower than their husbands. The present data, however, yielded a figure for what could be called the "underload" of non-employed wives compared to their husbands which is considerably larger than that in any previous study. One possibility is that full-time homemakers are spending more time in educational activities and/or volunteer work than employed wives, and that if this time is taken into account, they are working as hard as employed wives. However, analyses testing this notion did not find it to be the case.

Other Analyses in the 1977 QES

In contrast to the 1975–76 STU, in the 1977 QES two-earner husbands report slightly greater total work time than do sole-breadwinning husbands. While two-earner husbands report somewhat less paid work time, their reports of significantly greater family time make their total work substantially higher. Table 2.7 indicates that wife-employed husbands' decreased paid work time hold true across all parental status groups, including families with preschool children.

In the 1977 QES, husbands report increments in their family work associated with wives' employment to a slightly larger extent for childcare than for housework. They report the greatest increases, both in proportional and absolute terms, in both categories when there are preschool children.

The role overload of employed wives relative to their husbands in the 1977 QES is clearly greatest among families with preschool

TABLE 2.7 Employed Husbands' Weekly Time Use (Hours/Day) in Family Work, Paid Work, and All Work by Wives' Employment Status and Parental Status: 1977 Quality of Employment Survey

Time Use Category	Youngest Child 0–5		Youngest Child 6–17		No Children in Household	
	WE	WNE	WE	WNE	WE	WNE
All Housework	2.08	1.88	2.15	1.81	1.82	1.63
All Childcare	3.58	2.68	2.10	1.99	.01	.04
All Family Work	5.66	4.55	4.25	3.80	1.82	1.67
Paid Work	6.34	7.02	6.63	6.89	6.55	6.73
All Work	12.00	11.58	10.88	10.69	8.38	8.30
N	62	166	96	136	99	133

NOTE: Rounding errors may cause slight discrepancies in sums.
WE = Wife employed.
WNE = Wife not employed.

children (Table 2.8). Both employed husbands and wives show much steeper increases in total work with preschool children in the 1977 QES than in the 1975–76 STU.

Note on other Demographic
Predictors of Family Work

Previous literature has also examined the effects of education and race on family work (Pleck, 1983). Data on the relationships between education and family work are presented in the next chapter.

The analysis sample of the 1975–76 STU used here included four black husbands and 11 black wives. The analysis sample of the 1977 QES included 29 husbands and 15 wives. Previous literature on family time use among blacks is so limited that it is worthwhile to note trends in the present data. In analyses controlling for family life cycle stage, education, and wives' employment status (for husbands) or own employment status (for wives), black husbands in the STU performed somewhat less family work than whites (.78 vs. 1.89 hours/day, p = .064); black wives did less housework (3.58 vs. 4.52). In the QES, black husbands reported less housework (1.69 vs. 1.84 hours) but more childcare (1.86 vs. 1.59). Black employed wives reported doing less housework (3.66 vs. 4.34 hours) and less childcare (2.26 vs. 2.65 hours).

TABLE 2.8 Employed Wives' Weekly Time Use (Hours/Day) in Family Work, Paid Work, and All Work by Parental Status: 1977 Quality of Employment Survey

Time Use Category	Youngest Child 0–5	Youngest Child 6–17	No Children in Household
All Housework	4.79	4.57	3.72
All Childcare	5.40	3.56	0.00
All Family Work	10.19	8.13	3.72
Paid Work	5.36	5.51	5.89
All Work	15.55	13.63	9.61
N	56	81	83

NOTE: Rounding errors may cause slight discrepancies in sums.

DISCUSSION

The two surveys differ markedly from each other and from previous studies in their results on two fundamental questions concerning spouses' time when wives are employed: whether employed wives are overloaded relative to their husbands, and whether husbands do more family work in absolute terms when their wives are employed. The two surveys differ in several methodological respects which might account for the differences between them: measures of time use, and sample characteristics.

Most obviously, time use is assessed quite differently in the two surveys. Whereas the 1975–76 STU codes time use in paid work and the family from 24-hour time diaries for two week days and weekend days over the course of a year, respondents in the 1977 QES provided summary estimates for their time use in "home chores — things like cooking, cleaning, repairs, shopping, yardwork, and keeping track of money and bills" and "taking care of and doing things with your children" for working days and non-working days. Time use figures from the 1975–76 STU are subject to bias due to the possible nonrepresentativeness of the four days sampled; the subjective estimates of time use in the 1977 QES are vulnerable to various kinds of respondent bias.

A further difference in the time use measures concerns childcare. The "primary childcare" measure utilized here in the 1975–76 STU is quite restricted in its definition: activities codable as caring for, playing with, or helping children with homework in respondents' initial, unprobed descriptions of their behavior, and excluding many other adult activities in which children were recorded as present. By contrast, the 1977 QES's language ("taking care of or doing things with your children" when the youngest child was under ten, and simply "doing things with your children" when the youngest was over ten) undoubtedly included many activities excluded by the more restrictive definition used with the STU.

The two surveys also differ in the nature of their samples. As described earlier, using information from the four time diaries available in the 1975–76 STU necessitates rather restricted definitions of employment and non-employment. Specifically, to be considered as employed, husbands and wives in the STU had to be employed at all four observations during a twelve-month period and to have no paid work time on the weekend days observed; to be classified as not employed, wives had to be not employed at all four observations. As noted earlier, the high rate of change in wives', and to a lesser extent husbands' employment status, led to excluding a large proportion of the otherwise eligible sample. These necessary restrictions lead to a sample of two-earner couples which is probably quite unrepresentative of all couples in which both husband and wife are employed at a given point in time, though it probably does correspond to the popular image of two-earner couples. The 1977 QES, on the other hand, excluded both husbands and wives employed less than 20 hours per week, but did not require full-year employment or exclude those working on weekends. The full implications of these sample restrictions and sample differences for the issues being analyzed here are difficult to trace, but nonetheless may play some part in the two surveys' differences in results.

Our complex pattern of results, however, may not entirely be the consequence of methodological differences between the surveys. Perhaps each survey's results are valid in themselves, but pertain to a different aspect of the reality of the division of labor in contemporary American couples. Assuming for the moment that this is so, how could we describe and interpret that reality?

The starting point for our interpretation is to observe that the two surveys differ most in their figures for spouses' time in childcare. Respondents' estimates of their housework in the QES are 9 to 28 percent higher than the time diary figures in the STU, but their estimates of childcare are approximately 300 to 650 percent higher. While the QES estimates are high, they are quite consistent with estimates by parents and observers in a variety of smaller-scale studies in developmental psychology (Pleck, 1983). "Childcare", in reality, represents a continuum of activities ranging from intense, direct interaction, at the narrow end, to merely being available for interaction if needed, at the broad end. The coding of childcare behavior used in true time diary studies like the STU implies a narrow definition, while respondents' estimates of their childcare time appear to assess the broader end of the continuum. Neither estimate is more accurate than the other; they are both valid for describing different levels of childcare interaction, and are useful for different purposes.

Robinson's (1977a) analysis of what he terms "total child contact" in the earlier national time diary study, the 1965–66 Study of Americans' Use of Time, provides data consistent with this interpretation. For each activity, respondents recorded who else was present during the activity; it was thus possible to tabulate the amount of time spent in all activities during which a child was present, whether or not childcare, narrowly defined, was the primary activity engaged in. For similar subgroups, there is close correspondence between total child contact in this study (Robinson, 1966a, Table 3.8) and respondents' estimates of their childcare in the 1977 Quality of Employment Survey. For example, the figures for employed women in the former and employed wives in the latter (both groups including those without children) are 1.85 and 2.67 hours per day; for men and employed husbands, the figures are 1.91 and 1.61 hours. Due to the inclusion of non-parents in order to match comparable subsamples in the two surveys, these figures are not highly meaningful in their own right. However, they do suggest that respondents' summary estimates of their childcare involvement do roughly correspond with their actual total time spent with their children, though not necessarily in the direct interaction coded as "childcare" in diaries. (Unfortunately, the broader "total child contact" measure is not available in the STU data tape.)

If this explanation is accepted, then this chapter's results can be interpreted as follows: Employed wives continue to be overloaded relative to their husbands, but this overload derives from their spending more time being available to their children rather than extra time in housework and more direct kinds of childcare interaction. Husbands do respond to their wives' employment, but primarily in their time availability to their children, not housework and more narrowly defined childcare. (There is some precedent for the latter point in Robinson's (1977a) data from 1965–66. As noted earlier in this chapter, while the changes in husbands' housework and childcare were negligible, there was a somewhat larger increase in their total child contact, 19 minutes per day.) Husbands' increased time in more broadly-defined childcare is not enough, though, to lead to equality between husbands' and wives' total work loads in two-earner couples. When childcare is assessed more narrowly, however, then husbands do not appear to do more in the family when their wives are employed. At the same time, neither do employed wives appear to experience role overload compared to their husbands.

In effect, the nature of employed wives' overload and husbands' response to their wives' employment are both changing in subtle but important ways. The kind of role overload deriving from the combination of paid work and the narrower forms of family work, the form evident in the late 1960s and early 1970s, has diminished. But role overload due to the broader forms of family work remains. It is in this broader area of family responsibility that husbands of employed wives seem to be responding.

NOTES

1. As noted in Table 2.3 the time use means for husbands and wives classified by wives' employment status are adjusted, within sex, by Multiple Classification Analysis for differences in the distribution of respondents by parental status in the wife-employed and the wife-not-employed groups. This adjustment is necessary because the effects of wives' employment status are otherwise confounded by differences in parental status.

Childcare provides the clearest example. The unadjusted (i.e., raw or actual) mean time in all childcare by husbands of employed wives is .20 hours per day, .09 hours per day less than the unadjusted mean time of .29 hours per day for husbands whose wives are not employed. However, most of this difference in the unadjusted means is due to the fact that couples in which the wife is employed are less likely to have preschool children and more likely to have no children than are couples in which the husband is the sole earner. Adjusting for differences between the wife-employed and wife-not-employed groups on their parental status thus reduces the decrement in two-earner husbands' childcare from −.09 hours per day to −.01 hours per day. Table 2.5 provides direct data within parental status categories on differences in husbands' childcare associated with wives' employment: −.01 hours per day with preschool children; −.03 hours per day with school-aged children; .01 hours per day in couples with no children. These within-parental-status differences help show that the unadjusted mean difference of −.09 hours per day be misleading as an overall description of the effect of wives' employment on husbands' childcare, and that the MCA adjustment used here is needed.

2. Robinson (1977b, Table 4) reports an analysis of Wave 1 data for urban respondents in the 1975–76 study which found that employed wives spend 2.1 *fewer* hours per week in

paid work plus family work than do all employed husbands. The difference between Robinson's Wave 1 results and those reported here appear to be due to differences in the exact samples and coding categories used in each analysis, in addition to the sensitivity of weekly estimates based on single-wave data to the relatively small subsamples of weekend respondents in each marital group.

3

Paid Work, Sex, and Sex Role Ideology as Determinants of Family Work

As noted in Chapter 1, economists and sociologists have attempted to develop general theories of how individuals allocate time to family roles, especially in relationship to their paid work roles. Such analyses have become increasingly sophisticated. But there is a question that is often overlooked in studies of family time allocation. Why do husbands spend less time than wives in family work? This chapter does not claim to examine all the possible determinants identified in other research that would be necessary for testing a general theory of household time allocation. Rather, it considers a more limited set of factors particularly likely to be involved in the obvious disparity between husbands' and wives' levels of family, while controlling for basic demographic variables like family life cycle stage and education.

Previous research and writing offer two basic competing hypotheses for why husbands perform less family work than do wives. The first holds that men do little in the family because of the demands of their paid work role. The second argues, to the contrary, that the real cause is social beliefs, held by men but also shared by many women, that men should not be expected to do much family work.

The "paid work role" hypothesis can be expressed in two ways with quite different theoretical emphasis. The more traditional formulation of the paid work role hypothesis (e.g., Blood and Wolfe, 1960) views husbands' typical pattern of high amount of time on paid work and low amount of time in family work as resulting from differences in husbands' and wives' characteristic resources and skills, and as part of a larger pattern of marital differentiation that is appropriate and adaptive for the couple. Perhaps the most theoretically elaborate version of the traditional hypothesis is Scanzoni's (1970) argument that husbands, in effect, exchange their satisfactory fulfillment of their family breadwinning responsibility for their wives' performance of traditional female family role.

There is also a more radical formulation of the paid work role hypothesis. This argument holds that the demands of men's work role prevent them from exercising as large a family role as they should or would like to take, and which would benefit their families. Gronseth (1971), for example, has described males as being caught in a "breadwinner trap." In his analysis, all societies have to decide who holds the economic responsibility for the support of children. Western society has created the "husband economic provider role" as the socially sanctioned way of providing for children. But, argues Gronseth, filling this role prevents men from relating to their children emotionally. The traditional and radical versions of the work role hypothesis differ considerably in their implications — one viewing men as active and willing beneficiaries of the traditional division of family and sex roles, the other viewing men as passive and unwilling victims. But the fundamental idea which both hold in common is that men do little family work by virtue of their paid work role.

The second general hypothesis explaining men's typically low level of family work attributes this low level to men's traditional sex role ideology and sex role socialization. According to this hypothesis, men perform little family work because both they themselves and others do not view it as appropriate for them to do so. Further, traditional sex role socialization means that men are likely to have observed a traditional division of labor between their own parents, and are likely to have had considerably less prior training and experience in family work than their wives. The implication of this argument is that even if husbands' time in paid ~ ere reduced, men would not increase their time in the se of these ideological and socialization factors.

PAID WORK TIME

There are a variety of ways to evaluate these two competing hypotheses concerning men's paid work role and sex role ideology. First, several major studies find that men's performance of family work does vary significantly in relation to the time they spend in paid work (Blood & Wolfe, 1960; Walker & Woods, 1976; Robinson, 1977a, 1977b). This empirical relationship seems intuitively obvious.

Several studies, however, have questioned it on empirical grounds. Clark et al. (1978) has been widely cited as not finding such a relationship between husbands' paid work time and proportion of housework performed. However, several factors suggest this result may be idiosyncratic to this study and the measure of housework it used. None of the zero-order predictors of husbands' proportion of housework used in this study were strong, and husbands' paid work time was actually the second strongest of these (after wife's education). Also, a parallel analysis using the same data found that husbands' paid work time was significantly negatively related to men's childcare with young children (Clark & Gecas, 1977). Stafford, Backman, and DiBona (1977) found no significant relationship between men's paid work hours and housework in a sample of married college students. The relationship did appear, however, in a parallel sample of cohabiting students. In general, college students do not provide a good sample in which to study these relationships due to their unusual distribution of hours in paid work. Perruci, Potter, and Rhoads (1978) assert that their study finds no relationship between husbands' "time-availability" and their actual amount of family work. However, as indicators of husbands' "time-availability", these investigators did not use husbands' time in paid work, but used instead — curiously — the number of children at home, numbers of years of marriage, and husbands' age. Geerken and Gove (1983) report a correlation of only .02 between hours of paid work and hours of housework in 412 husbands drawn from a 1974–75 national sample, but this concerned husbands' time only on weekdays.

Thus, these four studies notwithstanding, the "paid work role" hypothesis for men's low family work cannot be faulted on the grounds that there is no empirical relationship between men's paid work time and their level of family work. However, two features of the precise nature of the empirical relationship between the two do suggest fatal flaws in the hypothesis. First, while men's level of family work does vary in relation to their time in paid work, this variation occurs around a low baseline which is *not* accounted for by men's time in paid work. One simple way to illustrate this phenomenon is to compare the amount of time spent in family work by women and men who are employed the same number of hours. If husbands' paid work time were sufficient to fully account for men's low family work time, then not only would the two co-vary significantly, but men and women with the same number of paid work hours would have the same family work hours.

The only time use study reporting levels of husbands' and wives family work for specific levels of paid employment is Walker and Woods (1976, Tables 3.14–3.15). The categories used for husbands' and wives' work hours are not, unfortunately, exactly equivalent. The closest comparison available is between wives employed 30 or more hours per week, and husbands employed 40–49 hours per week. The former perform 4.8 hours of family work per day, while the latter perform 1.7 hours, a differential of slightly over three more hours of family work for wives. More exact matching for work hours might reduce this differential to only two hours. But, even so, this differential is quite substantial. Something besides men's paid work hours accounts for this difference.

The second characteristic of the relationship between men's paid work and family time which undermines the "paid work role" hypothesis has to do with the exact nature of the trade-off between the two, i.e., exactly how much change in one is associated with how much change in the other. Robinson (1977b) finds that within the range of 20 to 60 hours per week of paid work, an increase (or decrease) of one hour of paid work is associated with a change of only 20 percent (i.e., 12 minutes) as much family work time. Thus, a decrease in men's paid work would increase their family work by a far smaller amount, suggesting that enlarging men's family role requires more than simply reducing their job hours.

From these considerations, we must conclude that while the demands of men's jobs clearly have a limiting effect on their family roles and account for some variation in males' family time, this variation occurs around a low baseline which is *not* determined by the demands of the male breadwinner role. This variation is far less than fully proportional to variations in the demands of this breadwinner role. The low baseline and low trade-off between male family performance and the work role must be accounted for by other, more ideological factors.

SEX ROLE FACTORS

A variety of studies have examined the relationship between measures of traditional sex role ideology and spouses' family work. Most of these (Hoffman, 1963; Bowling, 1977; Stafford, Backman & DiBona, 1977; Perruci, Potter & Rhoads, 1978; Roberts & Wortzel, 1979; Huber & Spitze, 1983) find significant associations between the two. However, many questions have been raised about this relationship. For example, both Bowling (1977) and Roberts and Wortzel (1979) note that these effects are quite small in absolute magnitude and relative to the effects of other predictors. Hesselbart (1976) found no significant relationship between either of two sex role attitude factors and Blood and Wolfe's measure of the division of housework between husband and wife in a broad community sample. Beckman and Houser (1979) showed a relationship between wives' sex role attitudes and their performance of feminine tasks, but not masculine ones. They questioned the importance of sex role attitudes in concluding that "despite differences among women in sex-role traditionalism and employment, most women say that they and their spouses divide tasks in a traditional sex role fashion" (p. 160). Geerken and Gove (1983) found weak and nonsignificant relationships between two sex role attitude scales and various measures of family work in husbands. Among wives, relationships were evident only among full-time homemakers, and were opposite to expectation: Traditional attitudes predicted a *less* wife-skewed allocation of responsibility. Huber and Spitze (1983) observed that the average of the husband's and wife's perception of the proportional division of household labor was significantly related to husbands' but not wives' sex role attitudes. When each spouse's report of the division of labor was analyzed separately, it was found to be significantly associated with that spouse's (but not the other's) sex role attitudes. In sum, while the majority of studies yield evidence of predicted relationships between sex role attitudes and level of family work, several investigators have commented on the low magnitude of the relationship, and a number of studies find either no association or relationships that are counter-intuitive.

Actually, these studies of the within-sex relationship between sex role attitudes and family participation provide a test of the sex role socialization hypothesis which is unduly restrictive. The real question is what sex difference remains in level of family work after the effect of paid work time is accounted for. The presence of sex differences in family work net of the effect of paid work clearly undermines the paid work hypothesis as the sole explanation of men's low family work. Introducing sex role attitudes as an additional predictor provides a further decomposition of this sex effect into an effect for sex role attitudes and an effect for sex remaining even after sex role attitudes are controlled. The results of this further decomposition contribute valuable evidence to our understanding of sex role attitudes and their utility as explanatory factors in sex-role-related behavior. But it is the combination of the sex and sex role attitude effects, not the latter alone, that tests the hypotheses that it is sex role factors, not paid work behavior, that accounts for husband-wife differences in family participation.

ANALYTIC METHODS AND ADDITIONAL MEASURES

Multiple regression is the primary analytic method used in this and later chapters utilizing ordinary least squares, including the use of "dummy" terms for categorical predictor variables. The regression coefficients reported here are always unstandardized (or "metric"). This means they represent the effect of a difference of one unit of the independent variable (hours, points on a scale) on the dependent variable, in actual units of the latter.

The study makes considerable use of multiple regression to test for moderator or interaction effects (e.g., work hours may have one effect on family time for husbands, but a different effect for wives), a procedure only beginning to come into common usage. House (1979) provides an especially useful discussion of this technique (see also LaRocco, House, & French, 1980, for an example). In brief, moderator effects are tested by including in the regression a term for the product of the moderator and the predictor variable(s) of interest. In the analyses here, moderator variables always have dichotomous categories (e.g., sex; high vs. low sex role liberalism). In this case, the product of the predictor(s) and only one category of the moderator need be entered. Through appropriate arithmetic manipulation of the resulting regression coefficients, the effects of the predictor variable can be calculated separately for each level or stratum of the moderator variable. Most important, the *difference* between the effects for each strata of the moderator variable (but not the significance of each effect in itself) is formally tested for statistical significance through this technique. Specifically, the inclusion of the moderator terms in the regression must lead to a significant increment in total variance accounted for (multiple R^2) compared to the identical regression without these interaction terms. If this criterion is met, then the significance of moderator effects involving particular predictor variables can be examined.

Following House's recommendation, the alpha (significance) level used for moderator effects and increment to R^2 due to interactions is .10 rather than .05, due to the inherent conservatism of the interaction testing procedure. When sex is used as a moderator (i.e., comparing the relationships between other variables among husbands and wives), the statistical significance of the within-sex coefficients is also presented, drawn from separate, within-sex regressions. When interaction effects are tested between strata within one sex, the within-strata coefficients in one sex are usually not formally tested for significance.

Measures

The analysis in this chapter used the indices of sex role liberalism that were available in each survey. While these measures are not identical, they are comparable. The indices in the two surveys in fact contain one item in common. The four items in the 1975–76 STU which were combined into a sex role liberalism scale were:

Most of the important decisions in the life of the family should be made by the man of the house.

There is some work that is men's and some that is women's, and they shouldn't be doing each other's.

A nonworking wife should not expect her husband to help around the house after he has come home from a hard day's work.

A woman who works full time can establish just as warm and secure a relationship with her children as a mother who does not work.

Respondents indicated their agreement or disagreement with each item on a five-point Likert scale. Scoring was reversed where needed so that high score represents liberal attitudes, and averaged across the four items. The resulting scale ranges from one to five. Coefficient alpha, a measure of a scale's internal consistency reliability, was calculated as .52 for males and .50 for females, values only moderate in magnitude. These questions were included in the third of the four waves of interviewing in the STU. In this survey, some error is necessarily introduced in analyzing the relationship of this attitudinal measure at one point in time to time use patterns aggregated over four points in time.

The 1977 QES included two sex role attitude items that were combined into a sex role liberalism index:

How much do you agree or disagree that it is much better for everyone involved if the man earns the money and the woman takes care of the home and children?

How much do you agree or disagree that a mother who works outside the home can have just as good a relationship with her children as a mother who does not work?

These items were scored as in the STU. The alphas for the resulting index were .66 for males and .58 for females, again values only moderate in magnitude.

Regression analyses in this and later chapters routinely include two major demographic variables: family life cycle stage and education. The form of family life cycle stage used here has five categories:

> 45 or under, no children.
> Youngest child 0–5.
> Youngest child 6–12.
> Youngest child 13–17.
> Over 45, no children.

In regression analyses, the "under 45, no children" group serves as the reference category with other categories represented as dummy variables, except in certain analyses involving only parents, in which "youngest child 0–5" is the reference category.

Respondent's education is coded in seven ordinal categories:

> 7th grade or less (some grade school).
> Grade 8 (completion of grade school).
> Grades 9–11 (some high school).
> Grade 12 (high school diploma, GED, or any high school equivalent).
> Some college.
> Grade 16 (college degree).
> Graduate or professional education in excess of college degree.

Finally, time in paid work is coded from the time diaries in the STU, but in the QES, is taken from respondents' estimates of their time at their main job plus time in second jobs, if any. All time use figures are transformed into hours per day.

EFFECTS OF PAID WORK, SEX, AND SEX ROLE IDEOLOGY

This chapter investigates the determinants of family work in three stages of analyses. First, the relative importance of paid work time, sex, and sex role attitudes as predictors of family work are examined in the pooled samples of employed husbands and employed wives within each survey. It is expected that sex has greater influence on family work than does paid work time. It should be noted that omitting housewives from the analysis in the 1975–76 STU (they are, of course, not available in the 1977 QES) restricts the analysis to those who have at least some time in both paid work and family roles. The inclusion of housewives, who have extreme "outlying" scores on both paid work and family time, would confound the interpretation of results.

Previous studies have examined the relationship between sex role attitudes and proportional measures of the marital division of family work. They make the same prediction for each sex: liberal attitudes are associated with a less wife-skewed allocation. Since the present study uses absolute measures of family participation for each spouse separately, it makes different predictions for each sex: liberal sex role attitudes are associated with increased family participation in employed husbands, but decreased participation among employed wives. These predictions are tested in a second stage of regression analyses using sex as a moderator variable. (In the first set of regressions in which husbands and wives are pooled, these two effects should cancel each other out.) Testing these predictions makes it possible to assess whether liberal sex role attitudes bring about a shift in the marital division of labor by increasing husbands' participation, by decreasing wives', or through a combination of both.

Previous research, as well as the analyses described so far, examine the overall impact of paid work time and sex role attitudes on family role behavior. The final part of the analysis goes further by investigating the notion that the time demands of the paid work role may have a greater negative impact on family time use among some groups more than others. It is predicted that work hours have a weaker effect on family participation among employed wives than among employed husbands. Interestingly, prior research does not appear to provide direct data on this issue, at least with absolute rather than proportional measures of family participation. As noted earlier, wives appear to reduce their family time relatively little when employed, and wives who are employed the same number of hours as their husbands nonetheless perform much more family work. These observations are consistent with the notion that for each incremental hour at the job, an employed wife will reduce her family time less than an employed husband will. This prediction is tested in the second stage of regression analyses in which sex is a moderator variable, together with the immediately prior prediction about the differential effect of sex role ideology in the two sexes.

It is also predicted that the paid work role will have a more negative impact on time in family work among those with liberal as opposed to conservative sex role attitudes. For husbands, the implicit notion is that among those with traditional attitudes, the real reason for their family participation is these conservative attitudes; variations in paid work time probably make little difference. But among husbands not having this traditional ideology limiting their family involvement, variations in the demands of the work role are a far greater determinant. Likewise, it is reasonable to think that employed wives will feel more comfortable reducing their family participation if they have liberal rather than conservative beliefs about sex roles. This prediction is investigated in a third stage of regression analyses, conducted separately within employed husbands and employed wives, in which a dichotomized form of sex role liberalism is a moderator variable. In all moderator regression analyses, in this and later chapters, the effects of basic demographic predictors (family life cycle stage, education and where appropriate, sex), are controlled for, though not shown in the tables.

Tables 3.1–2 present the first regression results for the two surveys. In both surveys, paid work and sex have strong significant effects on family work in the expected directions. High number of hours in paid work and being male depress family work, and housework in particular. As anticipated, sex role liberalism has a weak and non-significant effect in both surveys at this stage of analysis.

The magnitude of the effects for sex are substantially greater in the 1977 QES than in the 1975–76 STU. The magnitude of the effects for paid work are relatively more comparable in the two

TABLE 3.1 Metric Regression Coefficients for Net Additive Effects of
Background Variables, Sex, Paid Work Time, and Sex Role
Attitudes on Family Time, in Employed Husbands and Wives:
1975–76 Study of Time Use ($N = 352$)

	Family Time		
Predictor Variable	*All Family Work*	*Housework*	*Childcare*
Youngest Child 0–5	.519*	−.084	.603**
Youngest Child 6–12	.699**	.287	.411**
Youngest Child 13–17	.671*	.403	.268**
Over 45, No children	.145	.091	.054
Education (7 levels)	−.044	−.094	.049
Sex (1 = male)	−1.229**	−1.029**	−.200**
Paid Work Time	−.352**	−.308**	−.044**
Sex Role Liberalism	.155	.097	.058
Adj. R^2 explained by:			
Background Variables	.0127	.0206	.1867
Sex	.2992	.2811	.0770
Paid Work Time	.1828	.1830	.0309
Sex Role Liberalism	.0028	.0007	.0046
All Variables	.4975	.4854	.2992

* $p < .05$.
** $p < .01$.

surveys. In both surveys, approximately 50 percent of the
variance in family work is explained by the predictors used,
almost all of which is attributable to sex and paid work.

Tables 3.1–2 include summaries of the increment in adjusted
R^2 for the family work variables attributable to sex and paid
work time in the two surveys. As indicated in these tables,
sex accounts for considerably more variance in family work
than does paid work time. However, these estimates for incremental R^2 are contingent on the particular order in which sex
and paid work are introduced into the regression equations;
the present model introduced sex first. Since sex and number
of hours of paid work are strongly correlated ($r = 0.41$ in STU;
0.27 in QES), even when housewives are excluded, these two
variables necessarily share common variance in explaining
family work. This shared variance will be attributed here to sex,
since sex is entered first.

TABLE 3.2 Metric Regression Coefficients for Net Additive Effects of Background Variables, Sex, Paid Work Time, and Sex Role Attitudes on Family Time, in Employed Husbands and Wives: 1977 Quality of Employment Survey (*N* = 902)

Predictor Variable	All Family Work	Family Time Housework	Childcare
Youngest Child 0–5	4.212**	.710**	3.501**
Youngest Child 6–12	3.643**	.732**	2.911**
Youngest Child 13–17	2.070**	.390*	1.679**
Over 45, No Children	.377	.417*	−.040
Education (7 levels)	−.083	.026	−.110
Sex (1 = male)	−3.146**	−2.304**	−.84**
Paid Work Time	−.461**	−.238**	−.223**
Sex Role Liberalism	−.010	−.021	.011
Adj. R^2 explained by:			
Background Variables	.2434	.0076	.4322
Sex	.2063	.3259	.0429
Paid Work Time	.0488	.0430	.0248
Sex Role Liberalism	−.0004	.0013	−.0002
All Variables	.4981	.3778	.4997

* $p < .05$.
** $p < .01$.

To avoid this problem, Table 3.3 gives estimates of the common and unique variance attributable to sex and paid work in explaining each family work variable in the two surveys.[1] In the 1975–76 STU, paid work uniquely explains slightly more variance in family work than sex does. By contrast, in the 1977 QES, paid work uniquely accounts for relatively little variance in family work compared to sex, and relatively little in absolute terms. In both surveys, sex accounts uniquely for 10 to 15 percent of the variance in family work.

The difference between these results is consistent with the differences between the findings of the two surveys concerning employed husbands' and wives' patterns of time use noted in the last chapter. Employed wives in the 1977 QES reported substantial time in family work, in spite of their paid work schedule, while their husbands did not, thus leading to employed wives' reporting much higher total work time than did their husbands. In the 1975–76 STU, employed wives appear to show

TABLE 3.3 Common and Unique Variance of Sex and Paid Work Time as
Predictors of Family Time, in Employed Husbands and Wives:
1975–76 Study of Time Use and 1977 Quality of Employment
Survey

Survey and Family Time Category	Sex and Paid Work Time: Common Variance	Sex: Unique Variance	Paid Work Time: Unique Variance
1975–76 Study of Time Use			
All Family Work	17.6%	12.3%	18.3%
Housework	16.8	11.3	15.3
Childcare	3.9	3.8	4.1
1977 Quality of Employment Survey			
All Family Work	6.2	14.4	4.8
Housework	8.2	24.4	4.4
Childcare	0.2	4.1	2.5

TABLE 3.4 Conditioning Effect of Sex on Relationships between Paid Work
Time and Sex Role Liberalism on Family Time, in Employed
Husbands and Wives: 1975–76 Study of Time Use ($N = 352$)

Family Time (Dep. Var.) Independent Variable	Effect of Independent Var. when Sex Is:		Main Effect	Increment to Adjusted R^2 Due to Interactions
	Male	Female		
All Family Work				.0030
Paid Work Time[a]	−.297**	−.416**	−.352**	
Sex Role Liberalism	.213*	.033	.155	
Housework				.0006
Paid Work Time[b]	−.289**	−.332**	−.308**	
Sex Role Liberalism	.180**	−.049	.097	
Childcare				.0211*
Paid Work Time[b]	−.008	−.084**	−.044**	
Sex Role Liberalism	.034	.083	.058	

a. Conditioning effect of sex (i.e., difference between coefficients for males and females) significant at $p < .10$.
b. Conditioning effect of sex (i.e., difference between coefficients for males and females) significant at $p < .05$.
* $p < .05$.
** $p < .10$.

reduced time in family work commensurate with their paid work role. Thus, while paid work time uniquely explains relatively little variance in family time use in the QES, it explains relatively much more in the STU. Another factor is the restriction in variance in paid work time in the QES, due to the sample eligibility criterion of being employed 20 or more hours per week. This attenuation of variance necessarily depresses the effect of paid work time as a predictor in this survey.

Effects of Sex Role Ideology and Paid Work Time Within Sex

Tables 3.4–5 present analyses in which the moderating effect of sex on the impact of sex role liberalism and paid work on family time use is examined. In brief, there is only marginal evidence that sex conditions the effect of sex role liberalism on family

TABLE 3.5 Conditioning Effect of Sex on Relationships between Paid Work Time and Sex Role Liberalism on Family Time, in Employed Husbands and Wives: 1977 Quality of Employment Survey ($N = 902$)

Family Time (Dep. Var.) Independent Variable	Effect of Independent Var. when Sex Is:		Main Effect	Increment to Adjusted R^2 Due to Inter- actions
	Male	Female		
All Family Work				.0040[+]
Paid Work Time[b]	−.386**	−.731**	−.461**	
Sex Role Liberalism	.000	−.033	−.010	
Housework				.0015
Paid Work Time[b]	−.221**	−.294**	−.238**	
Sex Role Liberalism	.008	−.054*	.021	
Childcare				.0053*
Paid Work Time[b]	−.164**	−.436**	−.223**	
Sex Role Liberalism	.009	.021	.011	

a. Conditioning effect of sex (i.e., difference between coefficients for males and females) significant at $p < .10$.
b. Conditioning effect of sex (i.e., difference between coefficients for males and females) significant at $p < .05$.
+ $p < .10$.
* $p < .05$.
** $p < .10$.

work. In the 1975–76 STU, sex role liberalism is significantly positively associated with time in all family work and housework among males, while it has a near zero association to work among females.[2] The difference between male and female coefficients, however, does not attain significance. In the 1977 QES, sex role liberalism has a significant but low negative association with housework among employed wives, while it has a near-zero effect among husbands; again, the difference in coefficients is not significant, however. The hypothesis is born out in the limited sense that in both surveys, sex role liberalism has a relatively more positive effect on housework in husbands, and a relatively more negative effect in wives. However, the hypothesis is not supported in that sex role liberalism does not have a strong, consistent positive effect on family time use in husbands, or a strong, consistent negative effect among employed wives.

Results from both surveys also indicate that sex significantly moderates the effect of paid work on childcare and all family work. However, this conditioning effect acts in the direction opposite to the one predicted. It had been expected that because family roles are so strongly socially viewed as wives' responsibility, time in family roles would respond less to variations in job hours in wives than in husbands. In the present data, however, positive increments in paid work time lead to greater reductions in family work in employed wives than in employed husbands. One possible explanation for this finding is that employed wives spend more time in family roles to begin with. Thus, they have more room to reduce their family time in response to paid work time than do husbands. However, one could equally well argue that husbands have greater room to increase their family time if they reduce their work time, so this explanation is not entirely convincing. Another explanation is that wives may have greater variance in their work hours.

Effects of Paid Work Time Within
Sex Role Traditionals and Liberals

It was predicted that in both sexes, job hours will have a stronger negative impact on family time among those with liberal sex role attitudes than among those with conservative ones.

Tables 3.6–9 examine the conditioning effects of sex role attitudes on the impact of job hours on family work, separately within each sex.

For employed husbands in the 1975–76 STU, the hypothesis is borne out for housework. However, a significant moderating effect is found in the opposite direction for childcare. In fact, more paid work hours are actually associated with a slight increase in childcare among employed husbands with liberal sex role attitudes; the magnitude of the effect among both groups is extremely small, however. Among employed wives in the 1975–76 STU, job hours reduce all family work and housework significantly less among those with liberal as compared to conservative sex role attitudes, contrary to the hypothesis.

In the 1977 QES, paid work time has a less negative effect on time in family roles among those with liberal sex role attitudes among both husbands and wives, again contrary to our prediction. This moderating effect attains statistical significance only for housework among employed wives, however.

TABLE 3.6 Conditioning Effect of Sex Role Liberalism on Relationships between Paid Work Time and Family Time, in Employed Husbands: 1975–76 Study of Time Use ($N = 225$)

Family Time (Dep. Var.) Paid Work Time (Indep. Var.)	Effect of Paid Work Time when Sex Role Liberalism Is:		Main Effect	Increment to Adjusted R^2 Due to Inter- actions
	Traditional	Liberal		
All Family Work				.0019
Paid Work Time	−.269	−.362	−.302**	
Housework				.0116[+]
Paid Work Time[b]	−.242	−.391	−.293**	
Childcare				.0105[+]
Paid Work Time[a]	−.028	.030	−.008	

NOTE: Significance of coefficients not tested within traditional and liberal strata.
a. Conditioning effect of sex role liberalism (i.e., difference between coefficients for traditional and liberal groups) significant at $p < .10$.
b. Conditioning effect of sex role liberalism (i.e., difference between coefficients for traditional and liberal groups) significant at $p < .05$.
+ $p < .10$.
* $p < .05$.
** $p < .10$.

TABLE 3.7 Conditioning Effect of Sex Role Liberalism on Relationships between Paid Work Time and Family Time, in Employed Wives: 1975–76 Study of Time Use ($N = 127$)

Family Time (Dep. Var.) Paid Work Time	Effect of Paid Work Time when Sex Role Liberalism Is:		Main Effect	Increment to Adjusted R^2 Due to Inter- actions
	Traditional	Liberal		
All Family Work				.0138
Paid Work Time[a]	−.531	−.308	−.399**	
Housework				.0341*
Paid Work Time[b]	−.475	−.218	−.324**	
Childcare				−.0009
Paid Work Time	−.056	−.089	−.075**	

NOTE: Significance of coefficients not tested within traditional and liberal strata.
a. Conditioning effect of sex (i.e., difference between coefficients for males and females) significant at $p < .10$.
b. Conditioning effect of sex (i.e., difference between coefficients for males and females) significant at $p < .05$.
* $p < .05$.
** $p < .10$.

TABLE 3.8 Conditioning Effect of Sex Role Liberalism on Relationships between Paid Work Time and Family Time, in Employed Husbands: 1977 Quality of Employment Survey ($N = 685$)

Family Time (Dep. Var.) Paid Work Time (Indep. Var.)	Effect of Paid Work Time when Sex Role Liberalism Is:		Main Effect	Increment to Adjusted R^2 Due to Inter- actions
	Traditional	Liberal		
All Family Work				.0004
Paid Work Time	−.396	−.240	−.368**	
Housework				−.0003
Paid Work Time	−.229	−.156	−.216**	
Childcare				.0000
Paid Work Time	−.167	−.084	−.152**	

NOTE: Significance of coefficients not tested within traditional and liberal strata.
** $p < .01$.

TABLE 3.9 Conditioning Effect of Sex Role Liberalism on Relationships between Paid Work Time and Family Time, in Employed Wives: 1977 Quality of Employment Survey ($N = 217$)

Family Time (Dep. Var.) Paid Work Time (Indep. Var.)	Effect of Paid Work Time when Sex Role Liberalism Is:		Main Effect	Increment to Adjusted R^2 Due to Inter- actions
	Traditional	Liberal		
All Family Work				.0020
Paid Work Time	−.822	−.475	−.660**	
Housework				.0073
Paid Work Time[a]	−.406	−.142	−.286**	
Childcare				−.0014
Paid Work Time	−.411	−.328	−.374**	

NOTE: Significance of coefficients not tested within traditional and liberal strata.
a. Conditioning effect of sex role liberalism (i.e., difference between coefficients for traditional nd liberal groups) significant at $p < .10$.
** $p < .01$.

OVERVIEW

The analyses presented here provide the most detailed investigation to date of the relative impact of paid work time and sex role factors as predictors of time in family work. These analyses suggest several conclusions. First, in mixed-sex analyses, sex accounts for substantial variance in total family work time — between 10 and 15 percent — even when time in paid work is controlled. Second, sex accounts for much less variance in childcare than in housework time. Third, time in paid work also has substantial influence on family work time, but estimates of the degree of this influence vary markedly according to the range in paid work time in the sample analyzed. When individuals working less than 20 hours per week are excluded from the sample, as in the 1977 QES, the proportion of variance in family time uniquely accounted for by paid work time is much smaller than in the 1975–76 STU, which has no restriction on the minimum number of paid work hours per week among those classified as employed.

Three hypothesized conditioning effects were examined in analyses in this chapter. One was partially supported: liberal sex role attitudes have a relatively more positive effect on family work in husbands and a relatively more negative effect in employed wives. It should be noted that the strongest effect for sex role liberalism occurs among husbands in the 1975–76 STU. Its effects among employed wives in that survey, and among both employed husbands and wives in the 1977 QES are negligible. Since the measure of sex role attitudes is based on a larger and broader set of items and the assessment of time use is more objective in the 1975–76 STU, one is inclined to place greater weight on its results. Thus, one interpretation might be that while sex role liberalism increases family work among husbands, it does not depress it among wives, at least on the average. However, the more important point may be that the effects of sex role beliefs are simply neither large nor consistently replicated in the two surveys. In this respect, the results do not depart markedly from past research.

Two other conditioning effects were observed, but were opposite to what had been hypothesized. Variations in paid work have less rather than more impact on all family time and childcare in husbands than in wives. This result may have been due to the fact that employed husbands have a lower mean in their family work than do employed wives. Employed wives have more room than their husbands to reduce their family work in response to variations in their job time. Employed wives' greater variance in paid work hours may also be a factor. In any event, it is not employed wives with liberal sex role attitudes who reduce their family time most in relation to their job hours, but employed wives with conservative attitudes.

The second unexpected result in the investigation of conditioning effects was that in most comparisons, in within-sex analyses, variations in paid work time had less negative impact on family time among those with liberal than with conservative sex roles attitudes. A moderating effect in this direction occurred in ten of the twelve comparisons made. It attained statistical significance in three comparisons, two among wives and one among husbands (where the size of the effect was quite small). It had been predicted that job hours would have a relatively weaker negative impact on time in family work among those with conservative attitudes, because these attitudes dictate a traditional pattern of family role allocation that should be relatively insensitive to variations in each spouse's actual role in paid work. This predicted moderating effect occurred in only two cases, husbands' housework and total family work in the STU, and was statistically significant only for the former. (Interestingly, in both this and the previous analysis, husbands' housework in the STU is unique in demonstrating a predicted relationship to a significant degree.) A variety of interpretations are possible for this complex pattern of results, taking into account the differences between the two surveys in measures of both time use and sex role attitudes. Overall, there is far greater consistency in the results among employed wives than among employed husbands. In light of this, perhaps the most reasonable interpretation is that among employed wives, the work role has a more negative effect among those with traditional as compared to liberal sex role attitudes, while no clear moderating effect is evident among employed husbands.

Combining this result with the earlier one, it appears that time in paid work has a stronger negative impact on family time use among employed wives than employed husbands. Among employed wives, the negative effect is greater among those with traditional as opposed to liberal sex role ideology. As this implies, in Tables 3.6–9, the strongest negative coefficients in each survey tend to be for the traditional employed wives. Indeed, the regression coefficient for the effect of paid work hours on all family work among this group is $-.531$ in the STU, and an astonishing $-.822$ in the QES. Since the coefficients are unstandardized, in the latter case this means that an increase of one hour of paid work is associated with a decrease of .822 hours of family work, a trade-off approaching one-to-one, and the strongest relationship between the two variables in any study ever conducted.

In many ways, the finding in both surveys that the inverse relationship between job and family time is strongest among traditional employed wives is the most baffling result in the present study. It is quite counterintuitive. Several possible interpretations for it are ruled out either by other data from the analysis, or other factors. For example, this finding cannot be due to traditional employed wives having higher levels of family work to begin with. As shown in Tables 3.4–5, sex role liberalism has only a weak relationship with family work, though it attains statistical significance for housework in the QES. Traditional wives may be less likely to be employed if they have young children, or be less educated, but these variables are controlled for in the moderator regression analyses (though not displayed in the tables). Future research needs to explore the reasons for this particularly strong relationship between job and family time in this subgroup.

The ambiguities of the results on the interactions among sex, paid work, and sex role attitudes should not, however, deflect attention away from the more basic results of the analysis about why husbands do less family work than wives. Even if we accepted husbands' high work hours compared to wives as a given fact (which is, of course, logically indefensible, since it needs to be explained in its own right), it is clear that this fact is far from sufficient to account for husbands' lower amount of time in family roles. Differences in paid work hours account for some of the family time disparity between the sexes, but a large husband-wife gap remains even when work time is taken into account.

Of course, the number of hours spent at the job is not the only aspect of work schedules that affects husbands' and wives' time in the family. Staines and Pleck (1983) as well as considerable earlier research have shown, for example, that working other than the daytime shift is associated with increased housework in both husbands and wives. Husbands and wives in two-earner couples show similar rates of shift work, but there may be other aspects of work demands that are heavier for husbands than wives. Controlling for these possible differences may account for somewhat more of the husband-wife disparity in family work than does number of hours alone. But a strong sex difference will still remain.

Thus, a person's sex continues to exert a powerful effect on the amount of family work performed. But, sex role ideology does not have a consistent, strong effect on family work, both in this and other research. Why doesn't it make more of a difference? It may be that the concept of sex role ideology, as operationalized in surveys like those used for this study, needs to be fundamentally reconsidered. It has now become commonplace for surveys on the family and/or work to include a few items assessing sex role attitudes. Usually, there is not time for more than a few items, and the ones selected vary somewhat from one survey to the next, as exemplified in our two surveys. For many analytical purposes, these small, heterogeneous groups of items are probably sufficient, and one set is probably as good as any other.

In research focussing on more specific issues like the performance of housework and childcare, however, the current conceptualization and measurement of sex role ideology may not be as adequate. Items like those used here in reality tap a rather narrow range of sex role attitudes. This range might be characterized as varying from "extreme traditionalism" (e.g., an employed mother can't have as good a relationship with her children as a nonworking mother; the man of the house should make most of the important decisions) to "rejection of extreme traditionalism." But theoretically at least, there is a further ideological position, going beyond simply rejecting traditionalism, which involves accepting egalitarianism as a positive value. This more egalitarian view might be reflected by items like, "If a wife works on the job as many hours as her husband, he should spend as much time in housework and childcare as she does", and "Husbands should have as much responsibility for housework and childcare as wives do." While variation in attitudes between extreme traditionalism and its rejection might be expected to have some impact on an individual's family work, the greater impact of sex role ideology more likely occurs in the range between rejection of traditionalism and embracing egalitarianism.

The reason items assessing the more egalitarian part of the theoretical range of sex role ideology are usually absent from large-scale surveys is not an oversight on the part of researchers. Rather, there is typically little variation in responses to such items in representative samples (put bluntly, the overwhelming majority of respondents disagree with them), and they do not appear to justify the time they would take in the final questionnaire. This technical observation perhaps points to a more conceptual one. The attitude that husbands really should not be expected to do much in the family remains quite strong and pervasive in American culture, so pervasive in fact, that it is not typically included in the standard sets of survey items that assess those attitudes related to sex roles which show a reasonable amount of variation in representative samples. As a result, the relatively weak relationship of these latter "sex role attitudes" to family work time, both in this and other research, may be deceptive. There may well be an ideological basis for men's low family work, but it is simply not adequately tapped by current measures of sex role attitudes.

NOTES

1. A variable's unique variance is the increment it adds to R^2 when entered last in the regression. In the two-variable case, the increment to R^2 for the variable entered before the last variable is the sum of its unique variance and the variance it shares in common with the other predictor. Calculating unique and common variances requires comparing the results of regressions with different predictors entered last.

2. The coefficients for the main effects of paid work for each sex in Tables 3.6–9 differ from those in the "male" and "female" columns of Tables 3.4–5 because the former were main effects in within-sex regressions, whereas the latter were calculated from moderator regressions.

4

Wives' Desire for Greater Husband Participation in Family Work

In the previous chapter, we concluded that sex role ideology, as usually conceptualized and assessed, taps a relatively narrow range of attitudes. This attitudinal continuum does not as yet go so far as to include the view that husbands have as much responsibility for family work as do wives. Fortunately, the two surveys used in this study asked wives specifically whether they wish their husbands would perform more housework and childcare. This chapter will consider to what extent wives want their husbands to engage in these activities more and to what extent husbands perceive this desire in their wives, as well as test hypotheses about the determinants of wives' wanting their husbands to do more.

Attitudes about husbands' family work have been investigated in a number of earlier studies. Harris (1971, p. 440), for example, reports data included in a 1970 national poll concerning whether men should spend more, less, or the same amount of time on various family tasks. Only 20 percent to 35 percent of the national sample of men or women believed that men should do either "much more" or "somewhat more" of a series of tasks such as cleaning up around the house, washing dishes, and taking care of the children. There was little difference between men's and women's responses. Yankelovich (1974, Tables 25–26) surveyed a national sample of young adults concerning the value they gave to each of a number of family-related characteristics in men. Being "willing to do household chores" was rated a "very important quality in a man" by 30 percent of the non-college sample and 35 percent of the college sample. The parallel figures for the item "handy around the house" were 31 percent and 17 percent. As in the Harris study, there were no apparent sex differences in these responses.

Thus, college youth place greater value on men's willingness to do general household work than on their ability to do only the traditionally masculine repair tasks, while non-college youth do not. However, this is due mostly to the decline in the importance of traditional male repair tasks with education, not to the increased importance of general housework. Further, the difference between the value college and non-college respondents give to males' willingness to do household chores is quite small, 35 percent compared to 30 percent. If one assumes, as Yankelovich does, that differences between non-college and college respondents' beliefs are a clue to the direction in which general social attitudes will change, it appears that attitudes about men's general household work are changing less than a variety of other aspects of men's family role investigated by Yankelovich (not reported here).

Slocum and Nye (1976) and Gecas (1976) present data on husbands' and wives' norms concerning who should do the housekeeping and childcare in a study of 210 families in Yakima County, Washington. Only 2 percent of husbands and wives thought the husband should be equally responsible for the housework as the wife. However, 69 percent of sole-breadwinning husbands and 83 percent of husbands with employed wives thought husbands should do at least some housework. The figures for the parallel groups of wives were lower. Only 23 percent of husbands felt husbands had equal or more responsibility than the wife to clean or feed young children, while the percentages of wives responding to this were 7 percent and 10 percent.

In national survey samples in 1965–66 and 1973, Robinson (1977a) asked wives "Do you wish your husband would give you more help with the household chores?" The percentage responding "yes" was 19 percent in 1965–66, rising only four points to 23 percent in 1973. Robinson shows that the low percentages responding positively and the low increase between the two surveys are not the result of the presence of the husband during the interview, overestimation of the husbands' housework, or an increase in wives' perceptions of the amount of housework their husbands did. Robinson et al. (1977) also analyze responses to this item in relation to demographic and other variables. The percentage of employed women desiring more help was somewhat less than a third in both surveys, and the percentage desiring more help among wives who reported that their husband gave *no* help during the preceding week (about a third of the sample) rose from 24 percent to only 35 percent over this period. Desiring more help was only slightly related to wives' education, ranging from 24 percent for grade school educated wives to 30 percent for college educated wives. The group with the highest percentage desiring more help, and the only group in which the majority expressed such a desire, was black women: 58 percent in 1973, rising from 35 percent in 1965–66.

Scanzoni (1975, pp. 34–44) distinguishes three factors in attitudes toward the husband's family role in a study of 3,100 husbands and wives in five Midwestern states in 1971. These factors are labelled problematic husband alterations, institutionalized equality, and traditional husband role. Most relevant to our analysis is the institutionalized equality factor, with two items stating that if the wife is employed, husbands should share equally in "the household chores such as cooking, cleaning, and washing" and in "the responsibilities of childcare." Scanzoni does not report exact percentages of responses to these items. His other analyses suggest that men support equal sharing of family work significantly more than women in two of ten comparisons (young non-Catholics and old non-Catholics) and significantly less than women on one of ten comparisons (older blacks). Non-Catholics support equal sharing less than Catholics, and blacks more than whites (consistent with Robinson's data). Education is moderately but nonsignificantly positively related to support for equal sharing, while age by itself has only a slight negative relationship to support for equal sharing.

In a 1974–75 national survey, Geerken and Gove (1983) asked wives and husbands, "Taking everything together, do you feel you do more than your share of household chores?" About 30 percent of the 468 wives in the sample responded affirmatively, across various subgroups defined by wife's employment status, family life cycle stage, and income. Geerken and Gove did not conduct formal multivariate analysis, but the pattern of results suggested no average difference in wives' responses by family life cycle stage. Paraphrasing their results, low income housewives are more dissatisfied than their working counterparts in the prechild and young child stages, but more satisfied when there are older children or children have left the family. High income wives are generally more satisfied with the allocation of housework when they are employed except in the young child stage, when about 33 percent of both types of wives are dissatisfied. Oddly, employed wives with a preschool child and low income report feeling they do more housework than is fair to a relatively small extent, only 22 percent. Across all groups, about 15 percent of husbands felt they did more housework than they should. The rate of dissatisfaction was particularly high (33 percent) among low income husbands of employed wives with a child over six in the home. Similar husbands with a preschool child reported a particularly low rate of dissatisfaction (only 5 percent).

Another national survey including items concerning husbands' family work is a 1976 Gallup survey of U.S. males described by Hunt (1976). Hunt reports that about half of the males surveyed believed that husbands should do as much housework and childcare as their wives if their wives have paid jobs, but that almost as many responded "none, or at most a little" or "he should help her out part of the time." In a 1978 national survey, Huber and Spitze (1983) report that 78 percent of husbands and 78 percent of wives stated that if the husband and wife both work full-time, "the husband and wife should share daily housework equally." In these two most recent national surveys, half or more supported men's equal sharing of housework and childcare, but this attitude applies only to the circumstance that the wife is employed.

This review of recent national and other large scale survey data on men's family work suggests several generalizations. First, only a minority of the population believe that, in general, men should do more housework and childcare than they are now doing. Estimates of the size of this minority vary from study to study, and depend on the exact item used or comparison made, ranging from a low of about 10 percent to a high of about 35 percent. Even among wives who report receiving no help from their husbands, only 35 percent say they want more help. Only when the situation is posed more specifically that the wife is employed do half or more of the most recent samples surveyed support equal sharing of housework and childcare. Put simply, there is no consensus among either men or women that men should increase their family work.

Second, attitudes about men's family work seem to be changing slowly. Robinson's comparison of responses in 1965–66 and 1973 shows only marginal change, and in Robinson's and other studies the relationship between positive attitudes toward men's family work and age and education are rather small. Insofar as the size and direction of differences in attitudes by age and education categories suggests how attitudes will change over time, it appears that attitudes towards men's family work will change rather slowly.

Finally, three of the studies in which direct sex comparisons are possible (Yankelovich, 1974; Harris, 1971; Huber & Spitze, 1983) show no substantial differences between women's and men's attitudes; one finds more comparisons in which men hold more positive attitudes to men's family work than women do (Scanzoni, 1975); and one uniformly finds men holding more positive attitudes than women (Gecas, 1976; Slocum & Nye, 1976). Safilios-Rothschild (1972) also reviews a number of older and small-scale studies suggesting that women want or expect men to perform less housework and childcare than men want or expect themselves to perform. The margins of difference between the sexes are, of course, not great, and they are not always found. But they do suggest a need for future research into the reasons why women, often more than men themselves, resist an expansion of men's family role. It may be that women have a considerable psychological investment in their relative monopolization of family roles, and at least in some cases, become psychologically threatened if their husbands move into this domain.

In the following analysis, we first consider the extent to which wives reported wanting their husbands to do more housework and childcare in the 1975–76 STU and the 1977 QES, according to wives' employment status and parental status. Husbands' perceptions of their wives' desire for greater participation are also examined in the latter survey.

The determinants of desire for greater husband participation among employed wives are then examined with multiple regression methods. It is predicted that desire for husband help is associated with high family work participation by employed wives themselves and by liberal sex role attitudes. It is further predicted that sex role attitudes condition the effect of employed wives' level of family work on their desire for greater husband participation: High levels of family work are more strongly associated with desire for greater husband participation among employed wives with liberal as opposed to conservative sex role attitudes. Finally, we examine the impact of husbands' time in family roles on wives' desires for greater participation, as reported by husbands. Comparing this analysis with the earlier one permits us to investigate whether a wife's wanting greater participation by her husband is caused more by the wife's level of family work being high, more by the husbands' level being low, or equally by both.

DESIRE FOR GREATER HUSBAND PARTICIPATION

In the 1975–76 STU, wives were asked, "Do you wish your husband would give you more help with the household chores?" In the analysis here, responses were coded yes = 1 and no = 0. Wives with minor children were asked, "Do you wish your husband would give you more help with the children?", with the same response categories and scoring as for the housework question. These questions appeared in the third of the four STU interviews.

In the 1977 QES, wives were asked, "Do you wish your husband would spend more time on home chores, less time, or about the same amount of time on home chores?" In the analysis of this and related items here, more was coded 2, the same 1, and less 0. Wives with children aged 17 or under were also asked, "Do you wish your husband would spend more time (taking care of or) doing things with your child(ren), less time, or about the same amount of time?" The phrase "taking care of" was included if the youngest child was aged six or less, and the singular or plural form was used as appropriate. Husbands were also asked about their perceptions of their wives' desires, with parallel items beginning "Does your wife wish you would spend more time . . ."

Tables 4.1–2 present results from the two surveys concerning wives' desire for greater husband participation. About a third of employed wives in both surveys desire greater involvement by their husbands in housework: 34.1 percent in the STU, and 36.2 percent in the QES. The proportions of employed wives wanting more husband participation in childcare, however, differ markedly: only 22.5 percent in the STU, but 41.7 percent in the QES.

In the 1975–76 STU, employed wives want more husband help with housework significantly more often than do non-employed wives. This tendency is apparent with all parental status subgroups, though it is most dramatic and attains statistical significance only among those whose youngest child is of school age. By contrast, desire for greater husband help with the children is actually nonsignificantly more frequent among housewives than among employed wives. Comparisons within subgroups indicate a reversal according to age of youngest child: Housewives, more than employed wives, want help with childcare when the youngest child is aged 0–5, but employed wives want help more than housewives do when the youngest child is of school age.

Since the husband housework participation question in the 1975–76 STU was the same as that used by Robinson in 1965–66 and 1977, wives' responses can be directly compared with the earlier survey. Combining employed wives and housewives together, about 26 percent desire more husband help with housework, compared to 23 percent in Robinson's 1973 data and 19 percent in his 1965–66 data.[1] Robinson et al. (1977, p. 455) provide data on the desire for greater husband housework separately for employed and nonemployed wives for 1965 and 1973: 1965 employed, "almost a third"; 1965 nonemployed, 14 percent; 1973 employed, "almost a third"; 1973 nonemployed, 22 percent. Comparing these figures with Table 4.1 suggests that the increase in the percentage wanting more husband housework

TABLE 4.1 Wives' Desire for Greater Husband Participation in Family Work, by Parental Status: 1975–76 Study of Time Use (*N* = 283)

Desire for Greater Husband Participation in:	Employed Wives %	Base	Non-Employed Wives %	Base	Significance
Housework					
All Wives	34.1%	135	18.9%	148	*p* < .01
Youngest Child 0–5	39.3	28	29.5	89	ns
Youngest Child 6–17	34.0	53	6.3	47	*p* < .05
No Children	31.5	54	17.5	40	ns
Childcare					
All Wives with Children	22.5%	80	30.7%	114	ns
Youngest Child 0–5	25.0	28	41.0	61	ns
Youngest Child 6–17	21.6	51	17.7	45	ns

TABLE 4.2 Employed Wives' Desire for Greater Husband Participation in Family Work, by Parental Status: 1977 Quality of Employment Survey (*N* = 224)

Desire for Greater Husband Participation in:	Employed Wives %	Base
Housework		
All Employed Wives	36.2%	224
Youngest Child 0–5	46.6	58
Youngest Child 6–17	38.8	80
No Children	26.7	86
Childcare		
All Employed Wives with Children	41.7	139
Youngest Child 0–5	43.1	58
Youngest Child 6–17	40.7	81

is due to employed wives, who more often want help, becoming a larger proportion of all wives; the percentage of employed wives wanting more help appears to have risen only slightly, and the percentage of nonemployed wives wanting help has dropped slightly. However, these conclusions must be tentative since neither the analysis sample from the 1975–76 STU used here nor this simple examination of percentages is ideal for this comparison. Ideally, the full 1975–76 sample should be pooled with the two earlier surveys, using the method demonstrated in Robinson (1980).

Table 4.3 provides data on husbands' perception that their

TABLE 4.3 Employed Husbands' Perception of Their Wife's Desire for Husband's Greater Participation in Family Work, by Parental Status: 1977 Quality of Employment Survey ($N = 724$)

Perception of Wives' Desire for Greater Husband Participation in:	Wife Employed		Wife Not Employed		Signifi-cance
	%	Base	%	Base	
Housework					
All Husbands	54.5%	266	52.4%	458	ns
Youngest Child 0–5	58.7	63	59.4	238	ns
Youngest Child 6–17	59.4	101	51.4	138	ns
No Children	47.5	101	44.8	145	ns
Childcare					
All Husbands with Children	56.8%	162	52.5%	318	ns
Youngest Child 0–5	59.0	61	56.9	174	ns
Youngest Child 6–17	55.6	99	47.1	142	ns

wives want them to do more housework and childcare in the 1977 QES, asked in a format similar to the question posed to the wives themselves in that survey. Husbands with employed wives perceive their wives as wanting them to spend more time more frequently than do employed wives themselves in this survey: 54.5 percent vs. 36.2 percent for housework, and 56.8 percent vs. 41.7 percent for childcare. Interestingly, sole-breadwinner husbands report their wives want them to do more almost exactly as often as do husbands whose wives are employed.

Analyses not shown in detail here examine the relationships between desire for greater husband participation in housework and childcare among parents in the two surveys. While the two are significantly related in all samples examined, it is clear that desire for greater participation in the two domains does not overlap completely. In the 1975–76 STU, almost half of the wives who report that they want their husband to give them greater help with housework do *not* want him to help more with childcare, and vice versa. In the 1977 QES, about a third of wives desiring more participation by their husbands in one domain do not want it in the other, both in reports by wives themselves and in husbands' reports about their wives. Although it was initially hoped that the housework and childcare items could be combined into an index, the frequent disparity between responses to the two items made it clear that this was not feasible.

In results for the 1977 QES in Tables 4.1–3, wanting the husband to do less family work is combined with wanting him to do about the same amount. The proportions wanting less family work by husbands are small: among employed wives, 2.8 percent for housework and 0.7 percent for childcare; among employed husbands' perceptions of their wives' wishes, 3.1 percent for housework, and 1.0 percent for childcare. In the regressions reported in the next section, responses to these questions are used in uncollapsed form.

DETERMINANTS OF DESIRE FOR
GREATER HUSBAND PARTICIPATION

Tables 4.4–5 present analyses in the two surveys of the predictive effects of demographic variables,[2] family time use, and sex role liberalism on employed wives' desire for greater participation by their husbands in housework and childcare.[3] Surprisingly, almost none of the variables examined predict the desire for increased participation to a statistically significant degree, and the total variance accounted for is negligible. The one exception is that job hours predict desire for the husband to perform more childcare in the 1977 QES. Each additional hour per day of paid work increases the likelihood of desiring more husband childcare by about 7 percent. It is also noteworthy that sex role liberalism has no net effect on desire for more participation; in three out of four comparisons, in fact, its effect is nonsignificantly negative.

Several supplementary analyses were undertaken to examine a variety of possible reasons why the basic model yielded such weak results. First, further analyses in the 1975–76 STU added husbands' family and job time use as predictors of wives' desires for greater help. It might have been expected that husbands' time use would have a direct effect, and that wives' time use would have stronger effects when husbands' time use is included as a predictor (i.e., when husbands' time is in the predictive model, the effect tested for wives' time can be interpreted as wives'

TABLE 4.4 Metric Regression Coefficients for Net Additive Effects of Background Variables, Time Use, and Sex Role Liberalism on Employed Wives' Desire for Greater Husband Participation: 1975–76 Study of Time Use

Predictor	Desire for Greater Husband Participation in:	
	Housework (N = 121)	Childcare (N = 71)
Youngest Child 0–5	.162	——
Youngest Child 6–12	.097	−.023
Youngest Child 13–17	.071	−.250
Over 45, No Children	.003	——
Education (7 levels)	.096	−.065
Housework Time	.052	−.061
Childcare Time	−.091	−.039
Paid Work Time	.036	−.031
Sex Role Liberalism	.016	−.097
Adj. R^2 explained by:		
Background Variables	.0291	.0319
Time Use	−.0339	.0024
Sex Role Liberalism	−.0088	−.0023
All Variables	−.0136	.0320

spending much or little time relative to their husband). However, husbands' time use variables had no significant effects, nor did they change the predictive effect of wives' time use or of the model as a whole.

Other analyses in both datasets tested alternative models in which housework and childcare were entered as an aggregated family work variable, and in which family and job time use were entered as a single total work variable. These analyses were conducted to test the possibility that including housework and childcare simultaneously as individual variables was producing misleading results by, in effect, testing the effects of amount of housework (or childcare) which is high or low relative to the levels of childcare (or housework) or paid work. These alternative models were once again no more powerful.

Other alternative models were tested among the employed mothers in each dataset in which desire for greater husband housework and childcare were combined into an overall index of desire for greater husband participation in family work. These

TABLE 4.5 Metric Regression Coefficients for Net Additive Effects of Background Variables, Time Use, and Sex Role Liberalism on Employed Wives' Desire for Greater Husband Participation: 1977 Quality of Employment Survey

Predictor	Desire for Greater Husband Participation in:	
	Housework (N = 215)	Childcare (N = 155)
Youngest Child 0–5	.080	——
Youngest Child 6–12	−.072	−.176
Youngest Child 13–17	.222	.023
Over 45, No Children	−.188	——
Education (7 levels)	−.009	−.033
Housework Time	.012	.007
Childcare Time	−.004	−.024
Paid Work Time	−.005	.068*
Sex Role Liberalism	−.071	−.154
Adj. R^2 explained by:		
Background Variables	.0277	−.0027
Time Use	−.0111	−.0553
Sex Role Liberalism	−.0002	.0147
All Variables	.0164	.0673

* $p < .05$.

analyses were undertaken to examine whether the weak results in the original model resulted from the use of single-item dependent variables with highly restricted range (in the STU, only two points). This supplementary analysis likewise yielded results no stronger than those in the original model.

Finally, the predicted conditioning effects of sex role liberalism on the relationship between employed wives' time use and their desire for greater husband participation were examined. Contrary to the prediction that the relationship would be more strongly positive when employed wives' sex role attitudes were liberal as opposed to traditional, no moderating effects were found.

Table 4.6 examines the predictive effect of demographic, time use, and sex role attitude variables on employed husbands' perceptions that their wives want them to do more housework and childcare, in the 1977 QES. Statistically significant effects are found in the expected direction for husbands' housework and

TABLE 4.6 Metric Regression Coefficients for Net Additive Effects of Background Variables, Time Use, and Sex Role Liberalism on Employed Husbands' Perception of Their Wives' Desire for Greater Husband Participation: 1977 Quality of Employment Survey

Predictor	Desire for Greater Husband Participation in:	
	Housework (N = 665)	Childcare (N = 442)
Wife Employed	−.077	−.114*
Youngest Child 0–5	.083	——
Youngest Child 6–12	.011	−.139
Youngest Child 13–17	.134	−.119
Over 45, No Children	−.104	——
Education (7 levels)	−.022	.003
Housework Time	−.051**	−.019
Childcare Time	−.002	−.051**
Paid Work Time	.036*	.030
Sex Role Liberalism	−.054	.004
Adj. R^2 explained by:		
Background Variables	.0125	.0057
Time Use	.0286	.0493
Sex Role Liberalism	−.0003	−.0022
All Variables	.0408	.0528

* $p < .05$.
** $p < .01$.

job time on wives' perceived desire for more housework, and for husbands' childcare time on wives' perceived desire for more childcare. The less time husbands spend in housework and childcare, the more they think their wives want them to do more. While these effects are slightly larger in absolute magnitude than those found for employed wives, the much greater size of the husband sample in this survey clearly provides additional help in making these effects statistically significant. In absolute terms, for each additional hour a husband reports he spends in housework or childcare, he is 5 percent less likely to report that he thinks his wife wants him to do more of it.

DISCUSSION

The first important result of this chapter's analysis is that the proportion of wives desiring greater help by their husbands in housework in 1975–76 has continued to increase since Robinson's (1977a) surveys with the same item in 1966 and 1973. Nonetheless, it still remains a minority position — around a third. However, a somewhat higher proportion of husbands, a little over half, report their wives want them to do more.

A second important result is that almost none of the employed wives' variables successfully predict whether an employed wife will say she wants her husband to participate more in housework or childcare. In particular, neither employed wives' own time in housework or childcare, nor their sex role attitudes, are significant predictors. Desire for greater husband help appears to be independent of more general sex role attitudes, at least insofar as this can be determined by examining the empirical relationship between the two at one point in time. Nor do sex role attitudes play a moderating role in the relationship between employed wives' time use and their desire for husband help. In one of the two surveys, employed wives' time at their job is significantly associated with desire for more childcare involvement by the husband. However, this is the only relationship of a large number tested to be statistically significant, and it is not confirmed in the other survey.

Third, a wife's wanting her husband to do more, at least according to the husband's report, *is* significantly predicted by low time in family work in the husband. The domain in which the husband's performance is low exactly matches the sphere in which his wife wants greater participation: low amount of housework by the husband predicts the wife's desire specifically for more housework help, and the same for childcare. If one assumes that a husband's perception of his wife's preferences is reasonably accurate, then the second and third findings can be interpreted together with an important substantive meaning: wives want more family participation from their husbands primarily because their husband's level of family work is low, and not because their own level is high. If this finding is confirmed in other studies, it has important consequences for the way we conceptualize how patterns of the division of labor in two-earner couples lead to dissatisfaction in wives and its concomitants. This point is developed further in the next chapter.

It is also worth noting again the surprising finding that the measures of sex role attitudes used in these surveys do not appear to predict whether an employed wife will say she wants her husband to engage in more housework or childcare. While unexpected, this result is consistent with the preceding chapter's critique of sex role ideology, as currently conceptualized and assessed, in relation to family role behavior. We observed in that chapter's results that sex role ideology had no clear and consistent influence on wives' or husbands' levels of family work. It is possible that with different or better attitudinal measures, liberal sex role ideology would be found to predispose employed wives to want more help and moderate the impact of wives' own family time use on this desire, as originally predicted. Future research should also investigate a new possibility suggested by the interpretation presented above: A low level of housework or childcare by a husband may be especially likely to cause the wife to want greater involvement if her sex role beliefs are liberal rather than conservative.

The finding in this chapter that requires most discussion, however, is the first one. It will no doubt seem surprising to many that, though it is rising, such a small proportion of wives say they want their husbands to do more. It is clear that our results on this point are not unique to these particular samples, or to the specific form of the question asked in each. These results are consistent with those of a number of other surveys, using different question formats. The question wording in the STU might be faulted for its phraseology about the husband "giving you more help", implying that a husband's housework or childcare is just helping out and a gift to his wife, not a responsibility to his family. But the more neutral wording in the QES, concerning simply wanting the husband to spend more, less, or the same amount of time yields similar results for housework. For childcare, the item wording makes more of a difference. Nearly twice as many wives (42 percent) say they wish their husbands would "spend more time" with their children as say they wish their husbands would "give them more help" with the children (23 percent). These two phrasings for childcare have quite different connotations, much more so than in the case of housework. Apparently, a substantial group of wives appear to want their husbands to be more involved with the children because they think it would be beneficial to the fathers or children, over and above those wives who feel that they themselves need help.

It may be that these simple survey questions, whatever the wording, underestimate the true extent of wives' dissatisfaction with their husbands' family performance. If a wife wants her husband to to more, many factors may inhibit wives from honestly admitting it to a survey interviewer: the desire to "look good", the desire not to appear to be an oppressed wife. The approximately 55 percent of the husbands in the QES who say they think their wives want them to do more housework or childcare may more accurately reflect their wives' feelings than the wives themselves are able to report.

But even if the proportion of wives wanting greater household participation by their husbands is greater than the approximately one-third who say so directly, it is certainly not the overwhelming majority of wives. There are probably several different reasons why. Many wives may not see their husbands as very competent in housework or childcare, and they may indeed be right. In this circumstance, the husband doing more may actually create more demands on the wife, in the form of needing to train him or to deal with the consequences of his mistakes. Alternatively, wives may correctly observe that they and their husbands have different standards or values about housework and childcare. Getting the husband to do more might be perceived by these wives as increasing the likelihood of conflict between them. The relatively high frequency with which wives say they want greater husband participation in one sphere but not the other gives support to this notion. Wives' desires for more from their husbands do not simply reflect a global perception of satisfaction or dissatisfaction, but are at least partly a function of how they see their husbands in relation to a specific domain of family work.

Chapter 2's findings on the total work load of various subgroups of husbands and wives may also help explain wives' low rate of desiring more help. Since full-time homemakers perform less total work than their husbands on the average, it is understandable that they want more husband participation at relatively low levels, lower than their employed counterparts. In these recent data, employed wives' total work load is typically about the same as their husbands' when a narrow definition of childcare is used, though it exceeds their husbands' if the broader forms of childcare are included. Thus, it may not be surprising that even in this group, rates of desiring more help are rather low.

However, comparison of the 1975–76 STU results on wanting more help in employed wives with Robinson et al.'s (1977) earlier-cited figures for this group in 1976 and 1973 suggests that rates of desiring more help have stayed at roughly the same level even though employed wives' role overload, narrowly defined, compared to their husbands has declined. Likewise, housewives' desire for greater husband participation has apparently stayed the same while housewives' total work relative to their husbands has declined. Evidently, other factors besides the comparative total role obligations of husband and wife, specifically, larger cultural shifts in the standards against which husbands are being compared, affect whether wives will say they want their husbands to participate more in family work. Both groups of wives seem to manifest a "revolution of rising expectations."

Even though expectations are rising, the dominant attitude seems to be that husbands do not need to do more than they currently are. In addition to the other explanations offered so far, perhaps the most important reason for wives' low rate of desiring more from their husbands is wives' and the larger culture's belief that housework and childcare are ultimately wives' responsibility. In the 1977 QES, 74 percent of husbands and even 53 percent of currently employed wives agreed that "it is much better for everyone involved if the man earns the money and the woman takes care of the home and children." Many wives feel these domains are their "territory", and derive a sense of psychological identity from them. As long as wives have the major responsibility, these are also domains over which they have control, and which give them power in the marital relationship more generally.

It may initially seem incredible that employed wives could maintain this sense of territoriality, identification, and power even when overloaded relative to their husbands, as they so clearly were in earlier time use studies using a narrow definition of family work, and as they continue to be in the more recent data examined here when a broader definition of family work is utilized (the 1977 QES). But on reflection, it may not be so surprising after all. Consider how in previous decades, higher proportions of husbands felt that their wives should not work outside the home. Husbands persisted in this belief in spite of the fact that their wives' employment would have reduced the pressure on them as sole breadwinners and increased their family's standard of living. Husbands' socialized psychological identification with the breadwinner role, their proprietary sense about it, and the power they derive in couple relationship from monopolizing it, all seem sensible as explanations of why many husbands in the past (though fewer today) did not want their wives to work.

Parallel feelings about the homemaker and mother role may be evident in many wives. This is not to say that the only or most important reason husbands do not do more in the family is that their wives do not want them to. But our own results, as well as the findings of the earlier studies cited in this chapter (in many of which women have more traditional attitudes about men's family work than do men) make clear that husbands' typically low contribution to family work is not a state of affairs imposed by men on women, or serving only men's interests, in all or even the majority of cases.

This line of argument has been developed with some emphasis here because it is not one that has been widely expressed before. Perhaps this is because researchers have feared that such an argument might be interpreted as blaming women for men's low family work. But while stressing this interpretation, we should give equal attention to the fact that the overall rate at which wives report they want greater family participation from their husbands is slowly but nonetheless steadily rising over time, perhaps largely as a function of the increasing proportion of employed wives in the population. Further, the desire for greater participation is also becoming higher within both employed wives and full-time homemakers in relation to the actual comparative work loads for each group of wives and their husbands. Husbands perceive this increasing desire for greater involvement in their wives, perhaps even more clearly than wives themselves feel comfortable reporting to a survey interviewer.

Clearly, a major change in wives' attitudes is underway. In cross-sectional analyses within our samples, this new attitude does not seem to be directly predictable either from employed wives' level of household labor, sex role ideology as conventionally defined and measured, or their interaction. It can be predicted to some degree by low levels of family work by the husband. But whatever its sources, this new consciousness has already affected a substantial minority of wives, especially those employed, and will impact on even more in the future.

NOTES

1. In a separate analysis of the 1975–76 STU, Robinson (1980) reports a figure of 29 percent in this survey. The sample used in the present analysis differs from the larger sample Robinson used by excluding cases in which the wife had less than three complete time diaries or in which the wife or her husband changed employment status during the four waves of interviewing.

2. In the crosstabulations in Tables 4.1–3, parental status is trichotomized to maximize cell sizes; in the regressions in Tables 4.5–7, however, it is broken into five categories.

3. See Chapter 3 for a discussion of the "reference category" for family life cycle stage in the regression analyses in this section.

5

The Consequences of
Role Overload

When the role overload of employed wives relative to their husbands manifested in the time use studies of the 1960s and early 1970s was first noticed by researchers, it was interpreted not only as inequitable but also as having potentially negative consequences for employed wives' well-being (Meissner et al., 1975; Pleck, 1977, 1980). This notion of the adverse impact of role overload on the working wife became a relatively popular one in analyses of wives' employment. Actually, though, this notion is only one of many ideas about wives' employment and personal or family adjustment evident in past and present research on the topic. These other perspectives should be briefly noted, though the research related to them is far too extensive to review in detail.

Initially, the prevailing perspective was that wives' employment, since it violates traditional family role patterns, must negatively affect wives' adjustment. But the long line of literature on the effects of wives' employment on marital adjustment failed to find consistent negative effects in most subgroups examined and on most measures employed. When negative effects are found, they occur most often among wives in low prestige jobs or otherwise low in socioeconomic status, or when there are preschool children in the family (Staines, Pleck, Shepard, & O'Connor, 1978).

Then the idea arose that paid employment has positive effects, since it offers wives an alternative source of social and psychological rewards, helping to overcome the isolation and confinement which many perceive to be inherent in the housewife role. The critique of the housewife role's effects on women's mental health was first forcefully made by Gove (1972, 1979), and Bernard explicitly noted positive mental health correlates of employment for married women in *The Future of Marriage* (1972). Some recent studies (Kessler & McRae, 1982) continue to find that employment is associated with significantly better mental health in wives or women generally, while others do not (Pearlin, 1975; Radloff, 1975; Cleary & Mechanic, 1983).

In related theoretical analyses, Sieber (1954) and Marks (1977) note that many individuals like to work hard in several domains, and would suffer impairments of their well-being if they were *not* permitted to perform in several different roles. A recent line of studies on "multiple roles" (Stewart, 1978; Barnett & Baruch, 1979; Verbrugge, 1982) has explicitly tested these ideas by conceptualizing parenthood as a role distinct from marriage, and analyzing women's well-being in relation to simple number of roles (employment, marriage, parenthood) they hold. Using diverse indicators, these studies find that women's well-being becomes no worse or even improves with holding more roles. Of course, it could be that the direction of causality is reversed: having higher well-being may lead women to choose to take on more social roles.

The third general perspective on wives' employment is that it can be a source of stress. This perspective has much common sense to commend it, but it directly contradicts the equally sensible hypothesis that employment can provide psychological rewards. As Wright (1978) perceptively notes, feminist literature appears to simultaneously interpret employment as both the source of employed wives' better mental health relative to housewives' (as in Bernard, 1972) and as a source of stress. Like much other research (Staines et al., 1978), his own analysis of the 1971 Quality of Life Survey and several years of data from the National Opinion Research Center's General Social Survey finds only marginal differences in wives' well-being according to their employment status. In reality, employment creates both psychological demands and gratifications. Whether being employed increases or diminishes well-being for particular individuals or subgroups of wives depends on the balance of the two in their specific situation.

ROLE OVERLOAD IN CONTEXT

Against this theoretical and research background, where does the concept of "role overload" fit? Examining the relationship between variations in employed wives' patterns of time expenditure in paid work and family roles and their adjustment provides a way of partially disentangling the effects of the demands and gratifications generated by employment. Restricting the analysis to one employment status holds constant, at least to some extent, the element of psychological rewards from working. The total time expenditure required in work and family roles is clearly a major component of the stress which employment theoretically creates for employed wives. Analysis of the impact of variations in employed wives' time use would make it possible to isolate the effects of this stress. This kind of analysis could help reconcile the apparently contradictory ideas that while employed wives have as good or better adjustment than full-time homemakers, among employed wives a high level of total work has negative consequences.

In spite of the popularity of the concept of role overload in recent social scientific and feminist analyses of employed wives, there appear to be, surprisingly, no previous studies directly examining the relationship between employed wives' total work load (in job and family combined) and measures of their adjustment. A few available studies, however, do analyze the association between wives' or husbands' family work by itself and various aspects of wives' adjustment. Since wives' and husbands' level of family work are constituents or precursors of wives' total work, these studies are indirectly relevant. While they do not always focus on employed wives and their results are not consistent, these studies should be reviewed.

Considering first studies of physical health, Hauenstein et al. (1977) found no relationship between housewives' hours in housework (it is not clear whether childcare was included) and their blood pressure. However, there was a relationship among housewives between tension and critical self-evaluation about their housework and their blood pressure. Interestingly, the same relationship did not hold true among employed wives. Hauenstein et al. (1977) did not report analyzing employed wives' blood pressure and their time in housework alone.

In a second study, concerning mental health, Radloff (1975) found that husbands' and wives' reports of the numbers of times a week they "worked around the house and yard" were unrelated to a measure of depression. Examination of the data separately within husbands, employed wives, and housewives did not indicate a stronger relationship between the two variables within any of these groups. Radloff noted, however, that her measure of housework was a crude one. Respondents were classified as doing housework 0–1 times a week, several times a week, or every day. Most wives, both employed and not employed, fell into the last category (over 80 percent). The point at which excessive housework demands hypothetically start having negative consequences is probably not in the range tapped by these categories, i.e., not between "several times a week" and "every day." Rather, it is probably somewhere within the large category pooled together here as "every day." If so, it is understandable that this upper category did not reveal markedly higher depression than the two lower ones. Radloff further noted that depression was strongly positively related to having children, and particularly young children. She suggested that this variable must surely affect (or reflect) the amount of work done in the family.

In another study concerning depression, Pearlin (1975) developed a measure of housework "overload" in employed wives. This measure consisted of their reporting not having anyone who regularly helps them (it is not clear from Pearlin's description whether this referred only to paid help, or included husbands as well), having more to do than they can handle, having too little time for household jobs, and having no free time for themselves. Housework overload was significantly positively related to depression in employed wives. Pearlin (1975, p. 198) interpreted these data as indicating that "role strains result not because women prefer employment outside the home but because they experience severe demands in their employment inside the home."

Kessler and McRae (1982) reported a relevant analysis using data from the 1976 replication of the Americans View Their Mental Health Survey. In families with children of elementary school age or younger, the wife's employment benefited her mental health according to all five symptom scales considered if her husband spends equal or more time than she did in childcare, but had negligible effects if he participated less than she did. The nature of this interaction effect suggests that among employed wives, the higher the level of the husband's childcare, the better the wife's mental health.

Cleary and Mechanic (1983) studied depression in relation to wives' employment in a representative sample of adults in central Wisconsin. Among employed women but not housewives, having minor children in the household predicted depression. Further analyses indicated that this relationship held true primarily in the lower income subgroup of the employed wives, who were presumably less able to purchase household or childcare help. On the basis of this indirect evidence, Cleary and Mechanic (1983, p. 118) concluded that "among working women, the relationship between having children at home and depression is due partially to the time and work demands resulting from the dual role of being a working mother."

Three studies directly relate family work to marital adjustment. Bailyn (1970) found in a British sample that wives' performing more family work (as assessed by a housework frequency measure) was associated with lower marital happiness (on a composite index derived from both wives' and husbands' reports) among couples in which the wife was employed and had a positive attitude toward wives' employment. Gross and Arvey (1977) found no significant relationship between measures of both husbands' and wives' perceptions of husbands' relative task participation and wives' marital satisfaction. This relationship was not examined separately within employed and non-employed wives; however, Gross and Arvey did find an interaction between wives' satisfaction with the homemaker job and their employment status on their marital adjustment. Among employed wives, the two were positively related, while they were negatively related among unemployed wives. Wives' satisfaction with the homemaker job was not related to husband's relative task participation. Gross and Arvey's analysis is somewhat weakened by its use of relative rather than absolute measures of family work.

In an analysis related to but not reported in Staines, Pleck, Shepard, and O'Connor (1978), the investigators found that in a 1973 national survey, among employed wives with children, husbands' hours in housework and childcare (as reported by the wife) were positively and significantly related to wives' marital happiness. That is, less family work by husbands was related to wives' lower marital adjustment. The relationship was in the same direction but not significant for housewives. Unfortunately, this survey did not include data on wives' housework and childcare adequate to test directly the relationship between wives' total role demands and their marital adjustment. No information on family time use was collected from male respondents, and not even all wives were asked about their family time use.

In this literature, only one investigation (Bailyn, 1970) finds that employed wives' level of family work has a negative effect on their adjustment. Several studies do not, but their measures of family work are imperfect. Two studies (Staines et al, 1978; Kessler & McRae, 1982) observe that low family work in husbands, a likely correlate of high family work in employed wives, impairs the latter's well-being. A definitive test of the notion that role overload diminishes employed wives' adjustment is clearly called for.

Some previous research has also considered employed wives perceptions about their family work in analyzing the effects of the latter on adjustment. Moderating effects have sometimes been shown for such variables as critical self-evaluation about housework and satisfaction with one's role. However, earlier studies have not examined the direct or moderating effects of a more obvious variable: wanting the husband to do more. The present study will do this.

ANALYSIS STRATEGY AND MEASURES

This analysis provides the most direct test conducted to date of the impact of levels of time spent in family and job roles on the adjustment of employed wives and husbands. In past research, efforts to analyze the effects of time spent in family and work roles on adjustment have been confounded by the simultaneous goal of comparing employed and nonemployed wives. Since high amount of time in all roles combined is correlated with holding more roles, which may offer gratifications compensating for the stresses caused by high time expenditure, it has been difficult to isolate the effect of time use by itself. The present analysis attempts to test the effects of time use in work and family on adjustment more effectively by examining them with the number of roles occupied by the individual held constant. This is done by conducting the analysis only within employed wives, with the presence and ages of children statistically controlled. The analysis here includes an examination of the effects of employed wives' desire for greater husband participation in housework and childcare on wives' well-being, both directly and by moderating the impact of wives' time use. Our analysis also goes beyond prior research by explicitly investigating the effects of time use on adjustment among employed husbands.

In these analyses, three measures of adjustment are used: family adjustment, feeling of time pressure (feeling "rushed"), and global well-being. Measures for the first and last of these are similar but not identical in the two surveys, while the second was assessed in exactly the same way in both. For all measures, high score means good adjustment. Therefore, the measure of time pressure is labelled in the tables as "not rushed."

Items included in the family adjustment index in the 1975–76 STU were:

How often do you and your (husband/wife) sit down and talk with one another? (very often/often/sometimes/rarely/never)

How well do you think your (husband/wife) understands you — your feelings, your likes and dislikes, and any problems you may have? (very well/fairly well/not very well/not well at all)

And how well do you think you understand your (husband/wife)? (very well/fairly well/not very well/not well at all)

Generally speaking, would you say that the time you spend together with your (husband/wife) is extremely enjoyable, very enjoyable, enjoyable, or not too enjoyable?

Taking all things together, how would you describe your

marriage — would you say your marriage was very happy, a little happier than average, just about average, or not too happy?

Even happily married couples sometimes have problems getting along with each other. Would you say that this happens with you often, sometimes, hardly ever, or never?

Scoring was changed where needed so that high score indicates good adjustment. For the first item, "never" and "rarely" responses were collapsed together, and thus all items had four-point response scales. The resulting scale ranges from one to four. The alphas for this index are .75 for males and .78 for females. This scale was included in the third of the STU's four waves of interviewing.

Items included in the family adjustment index in the 1977 QES were:

Taking everything together, how happy would you say your marriage is? (extremely happy/very happy/somewhat happy/not too happy)

All in all, how satisfied would you say you are with your marriage? (extremely satisfied/very satisfied/somewhat satisfied/ not too satisfied)

(for respondents with children) All in all, how satisfied would you say you are with your family life? (extremely satisfied/very satisfied/somewhat satisfied/not too satisfied)

The resulting scale ranges from one to four. Alphas for this index were higher than .85 for both sexes.

In both surveys, feeling of time pressure was assessed by the item: "Would you say you always feel rushed even to do the things you have to do, only sometimes feel rushed, or almost never feel rushed?" Responses were coded one, two, and three, with high score indicating *not* feeling time pressure.

In the 1975–76 Study of Time Use, overall well-being was assessed by the single item "How do you feel about your life as a whole?" with a seven-point response scale (one to seven) with the categories delighted, pleased, mostly satisfied, mixed, mostly dissatisfied, unhappy, and terrible. This mode of assessing well-being derives from Andrews and Withey (1976).

The 1977 Quality of Employment Survey included Campbell

et al.'s (1976) Index of Well-Being. This has two components: general life satisfaction, measured by two overall satisfaction items concerning how happy the one is and how happy with the ways one is spending one's life; and a set of ratings of one's "present life" on eight specific moods or affects. The index is standardized to have a mean of zero. Quinn and Staines (1979) report the overall internal reliability of this measure as .87.

MAIN AND MODERATED EFFECTS

In the analyses in Tables 5.1–2, the effects of the time use variables on the three measures of adjustment are shown separately for males and females. In these tables, both the coefficients for each sex and the differences in coefficients between the sexes are tested for statistical significance, as well as the increment in R^2 due to sex as a moderator. The main effects for time use for the sexes combined are also shown. This analysis of the impact of time use on adjustment controls for the effects of family life cycle stage, education, and sex (not shown in the table). The time use variables are tested in different forms in three separate regression models: all work; family work and paid work; and housework, childcare, and paid work. These three models test somewhat different things, and it is useful to test all three. The coefficient for all work in Model 1 tests the hypothesis that it is the total amount of work from job and family combined that affects adjustment. The coefficients for family work and paid work in Model 2 test the notions that spending large amounts of time in family relative to one's job time, and large amounts of time on the job relative to one's family time, affect adjustment. Finally, the coefficients in Model 3 test the effects of each category of time use on adjustment relative to the time spent in the other two categories. Readers should be careful to note that in the text and tables, "all work" and "total work" refer to the sum total of time in paid work plus family roles. The terms "work" or "paid work" alone mean time in paid employment only.

In the 1975–76 STU, several significant effects appear within and between the sexes, all concerning family adjustment as the

TABLE 5.1 Conditioning Effect of Sex on Relationships between Family and Paid Work Time Use and Adjustment Measures in Employed Husbands and Wives, Controlling for Demographic Variables: 1975–76 Study of Time Use ($N = 334$)

Adjustment Measure (Dep. Var.) Time Use (Indep. Var.)	Effect of Time Use When Sex Is:		Main Effect	Increment to Adjusted R^2 Due to Inter- actions
	Male	Female		
Model 1:				
Family Adjustment				.0200**
All Work[c]	.050*	−.034	.013	
Not Rushed				−.0013
All Work	.021	−.036	−.004	
Well-Being				−.0029
All Work	−.012	.002	−.007	
Model 2:				
Family Adjustment				.0169+
Family Work[a]	.050	−.035	.009	
Paid Work[c]	.050*	−.034	.013	
Not Rushed				−.0042
Family Work	.035	−.036	−.000	
Paid Work	.018	−.037	−.005	
Well-Being				−.0026
Family Work	−.053	.024	−.008	
Paid Work	−.007	−.007	−.007	
Model 3:				
Family Adjustment				.0189+
Housework[c]	.046	−.079*	−.008	
Childcare	.078	.122	.093	
Paid Work[c]	.049**	−.034	.012	
Not Rushed				−.0060
Housework	.029	−.089	−.022	
Childcare	.084	.158	.106	
Paid Work	.017	−.036	−.007	
Well-Being				−.0030
Housework	−.060	.060	−.008	
Childcare	−.002	−.100	−.013	
Paid Work	−.008	−.007	−.007	

a. Difference between coefficients for males and females significant at $p < .10$.
c. Difference between coefficients for males and females significant at $p < .01$.
+ $p < .10$.
* $p < .05$.
** $p < .01$.

TABLE 5.2 Conditioning Effect of Sex on Relationships between Family and Paid Work Time Use and Adjustment Measures in Employed Husbands and Wives, Controlling for Demographic Variables: 1977 Quality of Employment Survey ($N = 900$)

Adjustment Measure (Dep. Var.) Time Use (Indep. Var.)	Effect of Time Use When Sex Is:		Main Effect	Increment to Adjusted R^2 Due to Interactions
	Male	Female		
Model 1:				
Family Adjustment				−.0008
All Work	.028*	.019	.024**	
Not Rushed				−.0011
All Work	−.057*	−.058**	−.057	
Well-Being				−.0004
All Work	.025	.010	.019	
Model 2:				
Family Adjustment				−.0015
Family Work	.035**	.021	.028**	
Paid Work	.013	.007	.011	
Not Rushed				−.0008
Family Work	−.014	−.045*	−.028	
Paid Work	−.155**	−.175**	−.160**	
Well-Being				.0008
Family Work	.016	.009	.014	
Paid Work	.052*	−.023	.036	
Model 3:				
Family Adjustment				−.0013
Housework	.020	.039	.026	
Childcare	.043*	.012	.030	
Paid Work	.011	.008	.011	
Not Rushed				−.0013
Housework	−.051	−.111*	−.073**	
Childcare	.022	.002	.011	
Paid Work	−.158**	−.175**	−.163**	
Well-Being				.0005
Housework	−.005	.018	.004	
Childcare	.030	.007	.023	
Paid Work	.050**	−.021	.036	

* $p < .05$.
** $p < .01$.

dependent variable. In sum, time in family and job roles has a relatively positive influence on family adjustment in employed husbands, but a relatively negative influence in employed wives. The differences between husbands' and wives' coefficients generally are statistically significant, and the coefficients within each sex attain significance as well, in several cases for males and in one instance for females. Of the various components of total work load, time in paid work has the most significant positive effect on husbands' family adjustment, though the effects for housework and childcare are also positive. In employed wives, time in housework has a significant negative effect on family adjustment, and the coefficient for time in paid work is also negative. The effect of childcare on family adjustment, however, is nonsignificantly positive, as it was for husbands.

In the 1977 QES, the results are more complex. As in the STU, time use in all categories is generally positively associated with family adjustment for husbands. In the QES, however, these effects attain significance for family work, and specifically for childcare. For wives in the QES, all categories of time use are nonsignificantly positively associated with family adjustment, and differences between husbands and wives in these relationships are not significant.

Similar results obtain for both sexes in the QES for the relationship between time use and feelings of time pressure. The more time spent in work and family roles, the more often both husbands and wives say they "feel rushed." While this effect is significant for all work combined, data in the table suggests it is due specifically to time in housework and especially paid work. The effects of time in paid work on time pressure are, in fact, the strongest relationships in the entire table. Time in childcare, however, has no overall relationship with individuals' sense of being pressed for time. Rather, it is paid work, and to a lesser extent housework, that makes people feel under pressure.

It is noteworthy that the relationship between feelings of time pressure and measures of time use reach significance and are far stronger in the QES, where time use is assessed with respondents' estimates, than in the STU, where it is assessed through the coding of diaries. This may indicate that individuals who report time pressure may tend to exaggerate their estimates of their time use, as a function of their subjective sense of pressure, even though their actual time use does not in fact differ from those not experiencing time pressure as assessed in diary records. If this is so, however, it is surprising that the relationship in the QES is stronger for time in paid work than for housework. Estimates of paid work time should be less vulnerable to perceptual distortion than estimates of housework, since the former occurs on a more fixed and regular schedule.

Finally, among husbands in the QES, spending time in paid work has a significant positive effect on well-being.

Tables 5.3–4 examine the direct effects of desire for greater husband participation in housework and childcare on adjustment

TABLE 5.3 Metric Regression Coefficients for Net Additive Effects of Employed Wives' Desire for Greater Husband Participation on Adjustment Measures, Controlling for Demographic and Time Use Variables: 1975–76 Study of Time Use

| *Desire for Greater Husband Participation in:* | *Adjustment Measures* | | |
	Family Adjustment	*Not Rushed*	*Well-Being*
Housework (N = 118)	−.272**	.188	−.426**
Increment to Adjusted R²	.0489*	−.0038	.0435*
Childcare (N = 56)	−.332+	−.175	.084
Increment to Adjusted R²	.0419	−.0127	−.0174

+ $p < .10$.
* $p < .05$.
** $p < .01$.

TABLE 5.4 Metric Regression Coefficients for Net Additive Effects of Employed Wives' Desire for Greater Husband Participation on Adjustment Measures, Controlling for Demographic and Time Use Variables: 1977 Quality of Employment Survey

| *Desire for Greater Husband Participation in:* | *Adjustment Measures* | | |
	Family Adjustment	*Not Rushed*	*Well-Being*
Housework (N = 217)	−.366**	−.229	−.727**
Increment to Adjusted R²	.0641**	.0043	.1190**
Childcare (N = 132)	−.501**	−.291	−.781**
Increment to Adjusted R²	.1445**	.0092	.1398**

** $p < .01$.

among employed wives, controlling for demographic and time use variables. It is evident from these tables that in both data sets, an employed wife's family adjustment and well-being are significantly lower if she wants her husband to do more housework and childcare than if she does not. These effects are quite substantial in terms of magnitude and of increment to multiple R^2, and are much larger than the effects of time use alone or time use moderated by sex.

Tables 5.5–6 consider the moderating effect of desiring greater husband participation on the relationship between family time use and adjustment among employed wives. In both datasets the desire for more husband childcare has a significant conditioning effect on the relationship of an employed wife's own childcare and her well-being. Employed wives' spending more rather than

TABLE 5.5   Conditioning Effect of Desire for Greater Husband Participation on Relationship between Time Use and Adjustment Measures in Employed Wives: 1975–76 Study of Time Use

Conditioning Variable *Adjustment Measure (Dep. Var.)* *Time Use (Indep. Var.)*	*Effect of Time Use When Greater Husband Participation Is:*		*Main Effect*	*Increment to Adjusted R^2 Due to Inter- actions*
	Not Desired	*Desired*		
Desire for Greater Husband *Housework (N = 118)*				
Family Adjustment				−.0084
Housework	−.060	−.058	−.060	
Not Rushed				−.0078
Housework	−.035	−.106	−.056	
Well-Being				.0094
Housework	.021	.011	.018	
Desire for Greater Husband *Childcare (N = 56)*				
Family Adjustment				−.0172
Childcare	.154	.216	.157	
Rushed				−.0128
Childcare	.024	−.474	−.042	
Well-Being				.0915*
Childcare^c	.177	−1.967	.055	

c. Difference between coefficients for desired and not desired groups significant at $p < .01$.
* $p < .05$.

TABLE 5.6 Conditioning Effect of Desire for Greater Husband Participation on Relationship between Time Use and Adjustment Measures in Employed Wives: 1977 Quality of Employment Survey

Conditioning Variable Adjustment Measure (Dep. Var.) Time Use (Indep. Var.)	Effect of Time Use When Greater Husband Participation Is:		Main Effect	Increment to Adjusted R^2 Due to Inter- actions
	Not Desired	Desired		
Desire for Greater Husband Housework (N = 217)				
Family Adjustment				.0041
Housework	.042	.057	.048	
Not Rushed				.0115[+]
Housework[a]	.013	.165	.075	
Well-Being				.0046
Housework	.016	.113	.055	
Desire for Greater Husband Childcare (N = 132)				
Family Adjustment				.0344*
Childcare[b]	.031	−.068	−.013	
Not Rushed				.0043
Childcare	.085	−.008	.043	
Well-Being				.0203[+]
Childcare[b]	.072	−.056	.015	

a. Difference between coefficients for desired and not desired groups significant at $p < .10$.
b. Difference between coefficients for desired and not desired groups significant at $p < .05$.
+ $p < .10$.
* $p < .05$.

less time in childcare has a negative effect on their well-being if they want their husbands to do more, but a positive effect if they do not. The same moderating effect of desire for more husband childcare holds true for family adjustment as well in the 1977 QES, but not in the 1975–76 STU.

The 1977 QES also reveals one counter-intuitive and uninterpretable conditioning effect. High number of hours in housework appears to reduce one's subjective sense of time pressure (i.e., has a positive relationship to not feeling rushed) significantly more among those who desire more housework by their husbands than among those satisfied with their husband's level of housework.[1]

THE DYNAMICS OF OVERLOAD

The first major conclusion from our analysis is that among employed wives, the amount of time spent in work and family roles, separately or combined, does not have strong or consistent impacts on family adjustment or well-being. In the STU, the effects of time use on family adjustment for employed wives are significantly more negative than these effects are for husbands. But the effects for wives are small in their own right, attaining significance in only one instance. These effects are not confirmed in the STU for the more global well-being measure, nor in the QES, where the time use variables generally have small, non-significant positive effects on family adjustment and well-being.

One possibility is that this discrepancy between the results of the two surveys is related to the STU's use of a relatively narrow definition of childcare while the QES uses a much broader one, as noted in Chapter 2. Perhaps employed wives' time in the broader category of childcare in QES provides psychological rewards which are sufficient to make the overall effect of time use positive in that survey. Direct comparison of the Model 3 results in Tables 5.1 and 5.2, however, does not support this possible interpretation. The effects of the broader childcare measure in the QES on family adjustment and well-being are quite close to zero (.012 and .007) while the effects of the narrower childcare measure in the STU are nonsignificantly positive (.122) in the case of family adjustment, though nonsignificantly negative (−.100) in the case of well-being.

The two surveys differ, of course, in other respects: the time use measures in the QES are more subject to respondent bias, and employed wives in the STU have to be consistently employed for a year. But there is no obvious link between these differences and the discrepancies between the results of the two surveys on the effects of employed wives' work and family role obligations. We are led to conclude that a high level of time in work and family roles does not impair adjustment in employed wives. As noted in the review of previous research, earlier studies offer relatively little direct support for the role overload hypothesis, so the results of the present analysis are not in fact dramatically inconsistent with them.

At least two interpretations are possible. First, part of the rationale developed earlier for investigating the relationship between time use and adjustment only within employed wives was that holding employment status constant would help disentangle the effects of the stresses and rewards generated by employment. These have been confounded in past studies comparing employed wives and full-time homemakers. It was argued that analyses within one job status would, to a large extent, control for the rewards of employment, while stress would vary directly with the level of total time expenditure. However, perhaps jobs (as well as family roles) provide both more stresses *and* more rewards as a function of spending more time in them. While high role participation may indeed cause more stress (as suggested by the findings on feelings of time pressure), it may also yield more psychological rewards. These two impacts might thus cancel each other out in employed wives' assessments of their family adjustment and overall well-being.

Another, not incompatible interpretation makes use of one of the main results of the preceding chapter. At least according to one measure of wives' dissatisfaction with the division of family work, desire for more participation by the husband, wives become unhappy not so much because they do so much housework and childcare themselves, but because their husbands do so little. If so, it is less surprising that employed wives' own levels of total work and its various components have no clear or consistent negative consequences on their adjustment and well-being. Rather, these negative impacts should be more a function of low amounts of husband time. The studies by Staines et al. (1978) and Kessler and McRae (1982) discussed earlier indeed confirm this effect. Unfortunately, the present study could not test this relationship directly, due to the limitations in the data on the family work measures available for spouses.

However, there is strong indirect evidence of this relationship in the second major finding in this chapter's analysis, concerning the main and moderating effects of wives' desires for greater participation by their husbands in family work. Among employed wives, wanting one's husband to perform more housework and childcare has extremely powerful direct negative effects on both family adjustment and well-being. Further, among employed wives, wanting one's husband to perform more childcare also moderates the effect of childcare on both family adjustment and well-being: high level of childcare reduces adjustment when greater husband childcare is desired, but increases adjustment when greater husband childcare is not desired.

In conjunction with earlier results, these findings suggest the following line of argument: The family time use problem in two-earner couples which has negative consequences for the wife is not her doing too much, but her husband doing too little. The latter causes the wife to feel dissatisfied with her husband and his level of family performance, which in turn directly diminishes the wife's satisfaction from the family and her well-being more generally. Further, dissatisfaction with her husband's level of family participation, especially in childcare, then causes the wife's own time in childcare to have a negative impact on her adjustment. It may be that employed wives performing high levels of childcare, who wish their husbands would do more, feel they have relatively little control over the demands made on their time by their children. For wives not wanting their husbands to do more, high amounts of childcare time may not be experienced this way, but rather more as the result of the wife's own choice. In this situation, childcare may provide more psychological rewards to the mother.

Altogether, these interpretations suggest some important modifications to the way that employed wives' "role overload" is usually conceptualized. In these data, a high expenditure of time in total work by employed wives creates a feeling of time pressure, but does not appear, in itself, to have direct negative consequences for them. This contradicts the intuitively plausible notions that a high level of combined job and family responsibilities is exhausting, and that this exhaustion must ultimately lead to adjustment problems. Perhaps the flaw in this hypothesis is that job and family roles also generate gratifications which compensate for the time pressures and fatigue. Perhaps when the pressure reaches the point at which negative consequences start to occur, individuals are relatively free to reduce their time investment in the job, family, or both. But whatever the reason, the intuitive overload-exhaustion hypothesis does not seem to be validated.

Rather than an "exhaustion effect" for the employed wife's own time, these data suggest an "inequity effect" for the wife's perception of her husband's time. Low family participation by the husband leads the wife to be dissatisfied with the division of labor. This dissatisfaction has direct negative consequences for the wife's adjustment and well-being. Further, when wives experience this dissatisfaction, their own childcare time contributes further to poor adjustment. This probably occurs not because when a wife is dissatisfied a given level of childcare is more exhausting for her, but because a given level of childcare feels more inequitable.

Thus, the potential issue in the dual-earner family seems to be that the husband's level of family work is too low, not that the wife's is too high. But what about the consequences of the husband's family participation on him? Would increasing it cause *him* to experience negative effects from role overload? The third major conclusion of our analysis is that a husband's time use indeed affects his adjustment. However, the direction of this effect directly contradicts the role overload-exhaustion hypothesis as applied to husbands. Total work time, and particularly paid work time has positive impact on husbands' well-being in the QES. In both surveys, higher levels of time use in work and family roles are associated with more positive scores on the family adjustment. Though there is some variation in which component of family and work obligations has this consequence to a significant degree on family adjustment in the two surveys, there is a general similarity of positive effects, especially for childcare.

Let us consider the implications of this finding in the context of the controversy in past research about the effects of wives' employment on husbands, and the role of husbands' time use in these effects (not reviewed earlier). Burke and Weir (1976) found negative effects for wives' employment on husbands' marital and life satisfaction, as well as a measure of physical and emotional health. The investigators argued that one reason for these consequences was the husband's "increase in his burden of responsibilities" (Burke & Weir, 1976, p. 285) in housework and childcare. Booth (1977, 1979) critiqued Burke and Weir's study for not controlling for age, which is a major predictor of well-being and health outcomes. In his own study, Booth observed no evidence of marital discord or health symptoms for husbands due to wives' employment. The same held true for family adjustment and well-being in two national samples examined by Staines et al. (1978), as well as the two surveys analyzed in this book.[2]

However, using data from the 1976 Americans View Their Mental Health Survey, Kessler and McRae (1982) reported that wives' employment is associated with depression and low self-esteem in husbands, even after a variety of other potential predictors are controlled for. Most interesting, though, was Kessler and McRae's discovery that these negative effects occurred more among men who did *not* take on childcare responsibilities than among those who did. (Housework did not have a similar moderating effect.) Childcare and housework were also tested as direct determinants of mental health in the pooled sample of husbands (no significant relationship), but not specifically within husbands of employed wives. However, the interaction effect involving childcare noted above suggests that in two-earner families, greater participation in childcare by the husband has a positive effect on his mental health. This is identical to the present study's results, which were particularly evident.

Thus, rather than having a negative impact, the dual-earner husbands' childcare and housework participation appear to have a modest positive effect on his adjustment. Why? One possible reason is that, just as for wives, these tasks may actually provide some gratifications among those who spend more than small amounts of time in them. Resentment from wives may also be a factor in the relatively poor adjustment of husbands performing little family work. This possibility is supported by the results already discussed showing that when husbands do little, employed wives want them to do more.

A third interpretation has to do with how, in the context of the time demands faced by the dual-earner family, actively participating in family work may provide the husband with a sense of control, a feeling that there is something he can do to respond to these pressures. Two-earner families clearly face stresses in getting the housework done and arranging for childcare. While husbands who perform low amounts of housework and childcare may have a low total work load, they also may experience low control over the situation. Housework needs doing and the children need to be cared for, causing stresses in the family, but the husbands do not perceive that they can do anything to relieve these stresses. In effect, husbands who do little housework and childcare experience "learned helplessness" (Seligman, 1974). By contrast, husbands performing more family work experience more control over their family situations. Whatever the reason, greater time in total work, especially paid work and childcare, has modest but clear positive effects on husbands' ratings of satisfaction and happiness with their family life.

To integrate the results for employed wives and their husbands: Limited participation by a husband in housework and childcare has modest negative effects on the adjustment of both husband and wife in dual-earner couples (cf. Kessler and McRae (1982)). The dissatisfaction generated in the wife by her husband's limited family performance seems to be the key mediator of its negative impact on her family adjustment and well-being. The dissatisfaction may have some role in accounting for the negative effects of low participation in family work on the husband himself. It is noteworthy that the factor that improves adjustment in the employed wife, higher husband family participation, also facilitates well-being in the husband.[3]

NOTES

1. The figures for the main effects of the time use variables on the adjustment measures in employed wives in Tables 5.5–6 differ from those in the "female" columns in Tables 5.1–2 because the main effect of desiring more husband participation is taken into account (not shown in the table), and because the analysis is restricted to those responding to the questions concerning desiring more husband participation.

2. Analyses not reported here in detail show that in the STU, employed wives differ from nonemployed wives in more often feeling rushed, but do not differ in family adjustment or overall well-being. No average differences on the three dependent measures were observed between husbands of employed and nonemployed wives in either data set.

3. Herrin (1983), appearing too recently to include in this discussion, contains many results relevant to this chapter.

6

Husbands' Psychological Involvement in Work and Family

The preceding chapters have investigated husbands' and wives' levels of family work and paid work in two-earner families, and their determinants and consequences. This chapter has a different focus: employed husbands' and wives' psychological involvement in their families as compared to their jobs. In particular, we examine the notion that males are much less psychologically involved in their family role than in their work role, whereas the opposite is true for women. While this view does not have a direct logical link to the family work issues we have considered so far, both are elements of a larger critical perspective on traditional sex roles and family life that has arisen in the last decade and a half as feminism has begun to influence both professional and popular thought. There seemed to be an implicit connection: Not only do husbands *do* relatively little in the family, but they also appear to *care* little about their families compared to their jobs.

There have been two major reasons for the perception that men have low psychological involvement in the family and high psychological involvement in paid work. The first is that it is easy to assume that actual behavior directly reflects psychological involvement or motivation. Since men obviously spend less time performing family tasks than they do in paid work, then it must follow — or so it is assumed — that their family lives are less psychologically involving to them than are their jobs. A second reason is the assumption that male and female sex roles must be mirror images of each other in all or nearly all respects. That is, if women are high on some characteristic, men must be low on it, and vice versa. Thus, if women are generally high on family involvement, then it must be — or so the argument goes — that men are low.

These two arguments initially seem persuasive — so persuasive, in fact, that many have not felt it necessary to look any further before concluding that men are indeed highly psychologically involved in their work and relatively oblivious to their families. There are, however, enough reasons to question each of these arguments to make it worthwhile to actually examine the relevant data. First, let us consider the concept of "psychological involvement" in a role or activity. This concept is used quite frequently in popular as well as professional discourse about individuals' behavior. The concept may seem to be an intuitively obvious one. The most explicit formal definition in past literature is provided by Gurin, Veroff, and Feld, using the term "personal involvement":

> The degree of personal involvement in the role . . . [is] . . . the degree to which the person's "self" is invested in it, how important it is to the person's life. This matter of involvement has implications for identifying how much and what kind of gratification a person expects from the role: a high degree of personal involvement implies he expects to gain from it an expression of the self and the satisfaction of personality and interpersonal needs. For example, satisfaction in a job that is seen as a major outlet of creativity and a source of major life gratifications is quite different from satisfaction in a job that is defined as the place one spends the day and earns the money necessary to find basic gratifications in other areas of life . . . The degree of involvement further suggests the extent to which a person seeks to validate the self in the role, the extent to which the role serves as an identity anchor, the extent to which inadequacies and problems in the role are experienced as ego blows. (Gurin, Veroff, and Feld, 1960, pp. 86–87)

Psychological involvement in a role (or the psychological significance of a role to an individual) *can* differ from the individual's level of role participation. Some activities can be very important to a person even though he or she spends little time in them. Conversely, some activities which a person spends a great deal of time in can mean relatively little to him or her.

The second reason for assuming that men's family involvement must be low is that men's and women's patterns of role involvement are thought to be the obverse of each other's. This argument may be suspect as well. There are many domains in which average differences between the sexes have been long thought to be both statistically reliable and socially significant. Current scholars, however, conclude that the sexes are far more similar in their psychological characteristics than they are different (Maccoby and Jacklin, 1974).

The same general finding holds true of the long line of studies of sex role "stereotypes." The apparent conclusion of these studies that women and men are perceived to be extremely different from each other (e.g., men are strong, women are weak) is now being reconsidered. It is true that on many (but by no means all) of the descriptive items used in stereotype studies, women and men are perceived to be different from each other to a statistically reliable degree. But on most of these items, men and women are perceived as being on the same side of the mid-point of the scale, and as similar in absolute terms (Spence, Helmreich and Stapp, 1974; Pleck, 1978). In other words, it is not really true that men are perceived to be strong and women to be weak; rather, men are perceived to be strong and women are perceived to be slightly less strong. The difference between the sexes is statistically reliable, but it is not large in any absolute case. As a result of these considerations concerning both average sex differences in other areas and so-called sex role stereotypes, there is reason to be skeptical of the assumption that men must, on the average, be low in family involvement and high in paid work involvement simply because women are presumably the opposite.

We will examine three kinds of data concerning men's work and family involvement. The first and most direct kind of data comes from studies using measures designed to assess work and family involvement themselves through direct self-reports. The second kind of data concerns the relative degree of satisfaction men get from their work compared to their family life. The theoretical relationship between role involvement and role satisfaction is complex. For our purposes here, it is sufficient to treat high role satisfaction in men as a corollary of role involvement. The third kind of data concerns the relative contribution of work and family role satisfaction to men's overall well-being. The assumption here is that the more psychologically involving a particular role is, the more of a difference satisfaction in that role will make to the individual's well-being.

EARLIER STUDIES

Levels of Work and Family Involvement

Dubin (1956) noted that previous theorists assumed that work must be workers' central life interest simply because workers engage in it so much. He argued that one could alternatively assume that holding employment simply indicates only that the worker performs above the minimal level justifying continued employment by his or her employer. Dubin developed a complex method to assess the extent to which work actually is workers' "central life interest", in comparison to other areas of social experience. He found that only 24 percent of the male employees in three Midwestern plants were job-oriented in their life interests. Dubin, Hedley, and Taveggia (1976), reviewing 19 studies of this type, found considerable variation in the extent to which work is workers' central interest in life, attributable to differences in occupational and organizational characteristics. Interestingly, work was found to be more of a central life interest of workers in the first female group to be studied, a sample of nurses (Orzack, 1959), than in the first male sample (Dubin, 1956).

Lein et al. (1974) conducted an intensive interview study of 14 two-earner working class and lower middle class families with preschool children. Lein et al. concluded that "men in contemporary industrial culture seek their primary emotional, personal, and spiritual gratification in the family setting. Many of the men in our sample showed greatest pride and emotion in speaking of their wives, the quality of their marriage or their pride in their children" (p. 118). In another intensive interview study, Farrell and Rosenberg (1982, p. vii) report that a major "unexpected finding is the discovery of the impact of family relations on the experiences of men entering middle age. Previous studies have emphasized the importance of work in male development. In fact, there seems to be a well-developed myth in our culture that men's emotional lives revolve around their work and are independent of their families. Our contact with the families demonstrated the ways in which a man's experience of midlife is very much dependent on the culture and structure of his family. The changing relationship to wife and children act as precipitants for development in men; at the same time, both wife and children are drawn into a man's defensive strategies, supporting his denial and avoidance of midlife issues. This interlocking of individual and family developmental processes is a critical element in men's experience in midlife."

Both Rosenberg (1957) and Adamek and Goudy (1966) found in college survey samples that expecting the most satisfaction in life to come from their "career or occupation" was more frequent in males than females. Nonetheless, many more males expected their greatest life satisfaction to come from "family relationship" than from work (62 percent vs. 25 percent in Rosenberg, 1957; 70 percent vs. 22 percent in Adamek and Goudy, 1966). The same pattern was revealed in another item in Adamek and Goudy's study concerning which role respondents saw themselves "primarily as a member of" when they looked to the future. Items used in a 1971 Gallup poll (Erskine, 1973) and in a youth survey by the Institute of Life Insurance (1974) concerning the "importance" of family and work further confirm this finding (cited in Hesselbart, 1978). In a follow-up of Terman's longitudinal study of gifted individuals, Sears (1977) found that men in this sample rated the family somewhat higher than work in response to the question: "How important was each of these goals in life, in the plans you made for yourself in early adulthood?" (Sears and Barbee (1978) present parallel data on Terman's gifted women, but unfortunately omit the involvement measures.) Veroff, Douvan, and Kulka (1981) also report a variety of detailed analyses in a 1976 national survey suggesting that men, like women, are far more psychologically involved in the family role than the paid work role.

The only apparent instance of data suggesting men are more psychologically involved in work than in the family is a single item in the Adamek and Goudy study concerning which role "a person can make his most significant contribution to society through", on which 56 percent of their sample of college males chose work compared to 41 percent choosing the family. Since this item referred to people in general rather than the respondent himself, it may be less useful as an index of involvement than the other items noted here. The finding that in all the other measures and studies reviewed, men report themselves to be less psychologically involved with work than with the family (though they are somewhat less involved with the family than women are) contradicts the usual stereotype of the male role as obsessed by work and oblivious to the family. The figures from the Rosenberg, Adamek and Goudy, and Sears-Terman studies are all the more dramatic when we realize they derive from college student or gifted samples, whose males are likely to be, if anything, more involved in work and less involved in the family than more representative groups of males.

Self-Reported Satisfaction from Work and Family

A second kind of data bearing on the relative psychological significance of work and family roles concerns the degree of satisfaction or gratification derived from each role. Campbell, Converse, and Rodgers (1976) found that marriage and the family were rated as more satisfying than work by both sexes, with few sex differences. Bailyn (1970), using a sample of husbands of British women university graduates (surveyed ten years after their wives' graduation), found that 59 percent listed "family relationships" as giving the most satisfaction in their life, while only 28 percent listed their "career or occupation." Sears (1977) found that men rated their satisfaction with their family higher than their satisfaction with the other five areas of life inquired about, with job satisfaction ranking third. The disparity between job and family satisfaction increased even further when the satisfaction ratings were weighted by the "importance" assigned each life domain.

Relative Contribution of Work and Family Experience to Well-Being

A third and final way to examine the psychological significance of work and family roles to an individual is to consider the relative contribution which satisfaction in each role makes to the individual's overall well-being.[1] Several different analyses on this point are available, using various kinds of measures. The most frequently used questions comprising these measures of "overall well-being" include: (1) "Taking all things together, how would you say things are these days?" (very happy/pretty happy/not too happy); (2) "In general, how satisfying do you find the ways you're spending your life these days?" (completely satisfying/pretty satisfying/not very satisfying); (3) ratings of one's "present life" on adjective scales such as interesting-boring, enjoyable-miserable, and worthwhile-useless (Campbell, Converse, and Rodgers, 1976).

Andrews and Withey (1976) found that, in multivariate analyses in combined-sex samples, family adjustment has a much stronger effect on well-being than does job satisfaction, with the latter's effect being practically negligible. There was apparently no sex difference in this pattern. Campbell et al. (1976, p. 85) report that for the sexes combined, family and marital satisfaction have a stronger relationship to global well-being than does job satisfaction. These investigators do not report conducting this multivariate analysis separately within each sex. They did observe, however, that earlier bivariate analyses found only small sex differences (p. 81).

Two studies have specifically examined the relative contribution of work and marital or family satisfaction to well-being within each sex. Using data from the 1973 NORC General Social Survey, Harry (1976) analyzed the bivariate relationship of job and family satisfaction to life happiness in men classified by family life cycle stage. In three of the five groups of husbands (preschool children, school-age children, and adult children), job satisfaction had a stronger bivariate correlation than did family satisfaction to life happiness. Morgan (1980) conducted secondary analyses of the eight-item semantic differential component (rating one's life) of the Index of Well-Being in the Campbell et al.'s (1976) 1971 Quality of Life Survey. She found that a work satisfaction index had a stronger effect on these life ratings than did a marital adjustment index, and that both relationships were stronger within males than females. Morgan's weaker results for the family role may result from using only marital satisfaction and not family satisfaction as the family independent variable, and from using only the semantic differential component of the Index of Well-Being.

In general, then, the preponderance of past research suggests that according to several different criteria — relative rankings of role involvement, satisfaction, and relative contribution to well-being — that men are more psychologically involved with their family role than their paid work role.

MEASURES OF INVOLVEMENT

Our analysis of wives' and husbands' psychological involvement in their family and work roles requires several measures in addition to those used so far in this study. These additional measures are available only in the 1977 Quality of Employment Survey, and the analysis thus uses only this dataset. It should be recalled that all the wives in the 1977 QES are employed. This might at first appear to limit the generalizability of the results. However, comparative analysis of the relative importance of family and work roles by sex does in fact require selecting samples of women and men who are engaged in both family and work roles. The additional measures used in this chapter are described below.

Family Role Involvement

Respondents were asked: (a) How often they thought about their spouse (and children, if any) when they were busy doing other things (always/often/sometimes/rarely); (b) How much they agreed or disagreed that the most important things that happened to them involved their marriage (or their spouse and children, if there were children) (strongly agree to strongly disagree, five scale points); (c) If they worked fewer hours per week, whether they would spend the extra time with their family, their free time activities, or equally with both; (d) Whether they would like to spend less time working so that they could spend more time with their spouse (and children, if any) even if it meant having less money. If they answered negatively, respondents were asked further whether they would like to work more in order to have more money, even if it meant spending less time with their spouse (and children). Combining these two items yields a single three-point scale: prefer more time, no change, prefer more work.

The fourth item has a weaker association to the set of items as a whole than do the other items. The first three items were averaged as a family involvement index, while the fourth was retained for analysis as an individual item. The alpha for the three-item index (.37 for husbands, .30 for wives) is lower than that for the other indices used here.

Work Role Involvement

Nine items were used as a work involvement index. The first pair of items parallel the first two family involvement items. The only difference is in the response categories for the "think about" items, which were always/often/sometimes/rarely for the family item, and often/sometimes/rarely/never for the work item. A second pair of items concern feeling that time "drags" at work, and putting effort into one's job beyond that which is required. The remaining five items were taken from a larger group of items in a job description sort, in which respondents sorted statements into five piles indicating strong agreement to strong disagreement: My job requires that I keep learning new things; My main satisfaction in life comes from my work; My main interest in work is to get enough money to do the other things I want; The work I do on my job is meaningful to me; and, I'd be happier if I didn't have to work at all. These items were selected through psychometric analyses of a larger group of 14 in the QES which had face validity as indicators of work involvement. The alphas for the resulting index were .682 for males and .743 for females.

It should be noted that the work involvement index differs in several respects from the family involvement index described above. Family involvement has fewer items, a lower internal reliability, and a narrower range of content than work involvement. It is likely that the lower reliability of family involvement is primarily due to its smaller number of items. In support of this judgment, the two indices have two items in parallel formats (*think about* and *important things*); these two involvement items are slightly more strongly correlated for family than for work (r for *think about* and *important things* = .29 for family, .24 for work, for husbands, r = .32 and .22, for wives; all p < .001).

Quinn and Staines' (1979, pp. 205–232) measure of Overall Job Satisfaction was used as the indicator of work adjustment. This measure is an equally weighted combination of a 33-item "facet-specific" job satisfaction series, and a five-item "facet-free" (i.e., global) job satisfaction series. The first of the latter group is an item exactly parallel to the global marital satisfaction item, which is part of the family adjustment index described in Chapter 5. The alpha for the work adjustment index is .85.

For comparisons of levels of involvement or satisfaction between work and family and relative work-family involvement or satisfaction between men and women, individual items are used since their exactly parallel wording facilitates such cross-domain comparisons. For most other purposes, indices are used.

LEVELS OF ROLE INVOLVEMENT

As shown in Table 6.1, on the first pair of measures of role involvement in identical formats for work and family, both wives and husbands clearly reported greater involvement in their family than in their work role. Seventy-five percent of wives and 65 percent of husbands indicated they think about their spouse (and children) when they are doing other things "often" or more frequently, while only 31 percent and 32 percent agree to the parallel statement about their jobs. These comparisons concern overall involvement in each role separately. Precisely the same pattern is evident, however, in analyses within each individual of the proportions reporting family involvement less than, equal to, or greater than, their involvement in work (Table 6.2). A majority of both wives and husbands indicated greater involvement in work than in the family. Sixty percent of wives and 55 percent of husbands report they think about their families more often than their jobs, and 74 percent and 60 percent rate the family more important than they rate their jobs. Only 7 percent of wives and 11 percent of husbands revealed less involvement in their families than in their jobs on either item.

TABLE 6.1 Distributions of Parallel Measures of Family and Work Role Involvement and Adjustment for Employed Husbands and Wives: 1977 Quality of Employment Survey

Measure	Employed Husbands		Employed Wives	
	Percent	*N*	*Percent*	*N*
Think about family[a]				
Always (5)	10.9%		14.1%	
Often (4)	53.8%		60.9%	
Sometimes (3)	31.3%		23.0%	
Rarely (2)	3.9%		2.0%	
		743		260
Most important things: Family[a]				
Strongly agree (5)	48.5%		55.5%	
Agree (4)	45.8%		40.2%	
No opinion (3)	1.4%		0.4%	
Disagree (2)	3.6%		3.9%	
Strongly disagree (1)	0.7%		0.0%	
		745		260
Spend extra time[a]				
With family (5)	50.9%		59.0%	
Equally family and free time activities (3)	27.1%		18.7%	
Free-time activities (1)	22.0%		22.3%	
		748		266
Work-family time preference[a]				
Prefer more family time (5)	40.3%		46.7%	
No change (3)	46.2%		48.0%	
Prefer more work time	12.4%		5.3%	
		738		258
Think about job				
Often (4)	31.9%		30.9%	
Sometimes (3)	35.3%		36.8%	
Rarely (2)	18.2%		20.2%	
Never (1)	14.5%		12.1%	
		750		267
Most important things: Job[a]				
Strongly agree (5)	15.5%		9.7%	
Agree (4)	39.5%		24.8%	
No opinion (3)	5.6%		6.1%	
Disagree (2)	33.1%		46.3%	
Strongly disagree (1)	6.3%		13.1%	
		748		267
Marital satisfaction[a]				
Extremely satisfied (5)	49.4%		37.5%	
Very satisfied (4)	41.8%		47.4%	
Somewhat satisfied (3)	7.7%		13.2%	
Not too satisfied (2)	1.4%		1.9%	
		745		261

Family satisfaction[a]

Extremely satisfied (5)	36.3%		22.3%	
Very satisfied (4)	53.0%		57.4%	
Somewhat satisfied (3)	13.4%		18.5%	
Not too satisfied (2)	1.7%		1.9%	
		493		156

Work satisfaction

Very satisfied (4)	49.1%		48.0%	
Somewhat satisfied (3)	41.0%		42.7%	
Not too satisfied (2)	7.4%		7.2%	
Not at all satisfied (1)	2.5%		2.1%	
		756		269

a. Sex difference significant at $p < .05$ or better.

TABLE 6.2 Within-Individual Comparisons of Family and Work Involvement and Satisfaction, for Employed Husbands and Wives: 1977 Quality of Employment Survey

Comparison	Employed Husbands		Employed Wives	
	Percent	N	Percent	N
Think about[a]				
Family less than work	11.2%		6.2%	
Family and work equally	34.2%		33.4%	
Family more than work	54.6%		60.4%	
		744		260
Importance[a]				
Family less than work	10.0%		6.9%	
Family and work equal	30.3%		19.6%	
Family more than work	59.7%		73.5%	
		742		260
Satisfaction				
Marriage less than work	2.9%		6.1%	
Marriage and work equal	52.5%		49.6%	
Marriage more than work	44.6%		44.2%	
		745		260
Satisfaction				
Family less than work	4.3%		6.5%	
Family and work equal	53.3%		55.4%	
Family more than work	42.4%		38.1%	
		493		155

a. Sex difference significant at $p < .05$ or better.

Wives' and husbands' family involvement is evident in the second pair of involvement items as well. Fifty-nine percent of wives and 51 percent of husbands indicate that if they worked fewer hours, they would spend the extra time entirely in the family, and 19 percent and 27 percent would spend it equally in family and leisure. Only about 22 percent of either sex would use the extra time entirely in leisure. The remaining involvement item, assessing desired reallocation of time between work and family (and reminding respondents of the economic consequences of any reallocation), reveals that a near majority of both sexes (46 percent and 48 percent) do not want to redistribute their time. Of those who did, however, many more would increase their time with their families (47 percent of wives and 40 percent of husbands) than in their jobs (5 percent and 12 percent) (cf. Best, 1981). On some of these involvement measures, employed men are less involved in the family and more involved in work than employed women are to a statistically significant degree. However, as in previous studies, these differences are surprisingly modest. The one exception was the endorsement of the statement that the most important things involve one's job (55 percent of employed husbands agreed, compared to 34 percent of employed wives). Thus, both employed married men and women report greater involvement in family than in work, though the margin of difference is somewhat smaller for men than for women.

LEVELS OF ROLE SATISFACTION

Table 6.1 shows results quite consistent with earlier research. Both wives and husbands report considerably greater satisfaction with their marriage (85 percent of wives extremely or very satisfied, and 91 percent of husbands) and family life (90 percent and 89 percent) than with their jobs (48 percent and 49 percent). When the distinction between "extremely satisfied" and "very satisfied" ratings are taken into account, employed married men report significantly greater marital and family satisfaction than employed married women, but about the same level of job satisfaction. Thus, both men and women report greater satisfaction from family than from work. The margin of difference of marital or family satisfaction over work satisfaction is greater for men than for women. By contrast, as discussed in the preceding section, the margin of difference of family over work involvement is somewhat greater for women than for men.

Table 6.2 further examines the proportions of individuals who report family or marital satisfaction less than, more than, or equal to their job satisfaction. The majority report work and family roles equally satisfying. When comparing their job to their marriage, 44 percent of wives reported the family more satisfying than work, and only 6 percent reported work more satisfying (for husbands, 45 percent and 3 percent). When the comparison was between one's job and one's family life more generally, the parallel figures were 38 percent and 7 percent for wives and 42 percent and 4 percent for husbands. Clearly, only a tiny minority of either sex report job more satisfying than either their marriage or their family life.

THE RELATIVE CONTRIBUTION OF WORK AND FAMILY ROLES TO WELL-BEING

Table 6.3 presents the results of a regression analysis of the impact of family and work variables on the Index of Well-Being, in the pooled sample of husbands and wives. After the effects of family life cycle stage, education, and sex are taken into account, family adjustment, work involvement, and work adjustment have significant predictive effects on well-being.[2] However, the regression coefficient for family adjustment is considerably greater than the coefficients for the two work role predictors.

Further, the proportion of variance in well-being accounted for by the family role variables (20.3 percent) is about twice as large as the variance attributable to the work role variables (10.1 percent). In this regression model, the family variables were entered as a group before the work variables. However, in an alternate analysis not shown here, the work variables were entered in the regression first, thus permitting the variance shared in common between the two groups of variables to be

TABLE 6.3 Metric Regression Coefficients for Net Additive Effects of Background, Family, and Work Variables on Well-Being: 1977 Quality of Employment Survey ($N = 912$)

Predictor	Effect on Well-Being
Youngest Child 0–6	−.197*
Youngest Child 7–12	−.022
Youngest Child 13–17	−.185
Over 45, No Children	.008
Education	.026
Male	−.148
Housework Time	−.011
Childcare Time	.010
Family Involvement	.064
Family Adjustment	.484**
Work Time	.000
Work Involvement	.307**
Work Adjustment	.239**
Adjusted R^2 explained by:	
Background Variables	.0170
Family Variables	.2028
Work Variables	.1009
All Variables	.3207

* $p < .05$.
** $p < .01$.

assigned to the work variables. Even in this alternate analysis, the family variables still accounted for more variance in well-being (16.9 percent) than did the work variables (13.5 percent).

Finally, Table 6.4 presents an analysis explicitly testing for sex differences in the effects of the three significant work and family predictors on well-being, net of the effects of the other predictors (not shown in the table). This analysis suggests that all three work and family variables have stronger effects on well-being in wives than in husbands. However, these effects are not significantly stronger, as assessed by the formal test of significance of the interaction between these variables and sex.

TABLE 6.4 Conditioning Effect of Sex on Relationships between Work and Family Predictors on Well-Being (Net of Other Predictors): 1977 Quality of Employment Survey ($N = 912$)

Well-Being (Dep. Var.) *Work or Family Predictor* *(Indep. Var.)*	*Effect of Work or Family Predictor When Sex is:*		*Main Effect*	*Increment in Adj. R^2 Due to Interaction*
	Male	*Female*		
Well-Being				.0004
Work Involvement	.281	.367	.307	
Work Adjustment	.221	.312	.239	
Family Adjustment	.483	.540	.484	

HUSBANDS, INVOLVEMENT, AND THE FAMILY

All three kinds of analyses indicate that wives *and* husbands experience their family role as far more psychologically significant than their paid work role. These findings are consistent with most earlier research, but the results for husbands will no doubt seem counter-intuitive to many readers. The first two kinds of evidence — self-rated psychological involvement in and satisfaction from the family — are, of course, subject to the criticism that they derive from self-reports, easily biased by individuals' tendency to give socially desirable answers. If these were the only data suggesting the pre-eminent significance of the family to men, they would be suspect. However, the third kind of data — the relationship between family satisfaction and overall well-being — is not vulnerable to this criticism, and affirms the conclusion provided by the self-report data. What is perhaps most surprising is that the view that most men are obsessed by their work and oblivious to their families has persisted so long in spite of the fact that the available data have almost always disconfirmed it.

This conclusion does not deny, however, that there is a minority of men who are more involved with their jobs than with their families. The studies cited earlier using samples of highly educated or high status men generally find somewhat higher work involvement and somewhat lower family involvement than is found in more representative samples. However, even in these highly educated samples, men who are more involved in their work than in their family are still in the minority. In our own data, there is a small percentage of men with greater work than family involvement, and they are doubtless over-represented among the more educated and occupationally successful. This group is certainly worthy of study (e.g., Masih, 1967; Burke, Weir, and DuWors, 1979). The important point, however, is that our general analysis of the male role should not be based on this group (as many previous discussions of the male role are), but rather should be based on the experience of more typical males.

Overall, this discussion leads to a conclusion which seems very difficult to accept, namely, that the majority of men are more psychologically involved in their families than their jobs. It is important to note immediately that this conclusion does not deny that men perform relatively little housework and childcare and is not necessarily inconsistent with it. Nor does it deny that there may be qualitative differences in the nature of psychological involvement in the family between husbands and wives. If fundamental differences exist in psychological involvement, they occur at a more subtle level than has been assessed in past and current research.

This conclusion does, however, have important implications for how one approaches the formidable task of enlarging men's family performance. Trying to increase men's family work when men's psychological involvement in the family is high is not the same problem as trying to elevate men's family work when their involvement is low. To put it another way, increasing men's family work when their psychological involvement is high is different than attempting to raise men's family work and family involvement simultaneously. To solve the problem, it is essential to diagnose it correctly. Most men's high degree of psychological involvement in their families provides a foundation for enlarging men's performance of housework and childcare, making this social task easier.

The misperception of the significance of the family role to men is particularly extreme in early writings on men's liberation. This literature developed a highly overdrawn portrait of men as obsessed by their jobs and oblivious to their families. This caricature represented a first attempt to identify a critical problem in male experience, and it described just enough men that it seemed to ring true for men in general. This overdrawn portrait was, of course, motivated by a desire to foster change in men by presenting a negative image of themselves that would stimulate them to change in a positive direction. This overdrawn image has now served its purpose; fostering future change in men requires an updated and more complex view.

NOTES

1. Rice, Near, and Hunt (1980) provide a detailed review of research on the impact of job satisfaction by itself on life satisfaction.

2. The regression coefficients for the effects of time in housework, childcare, and paid work on well-being in the QES in Table 6.3 differ from those in the "main effect" column of Table 5.2 because Table 6.3 includes role involvement and satisfaction measures as additional predictors.

7

Husbands' and
Wives' Roles:
The Issues Today

As discussed at the outset of this book, findings from time use research in the 1960s and early 1970s revealed fatal flaws in the traditional "resource" theory of the division of labor in the family. These time use data, interpreted in the context of contemporary feminism, led to a set of propositions about husbands' and wives' roles, especially in two-earner couples, which constitute the role overload hypothesis. This new perspective is far more critical than the traditional one of these role patterns and their consequences for wives.

In essence, the role overload hypothesis holds that the division of family work in two-earner couples, deriving from traditional sex role ideology and husbands' low psychological investment in the family, is inequitable, a source of conscious dissatisfaction to wives, and injurious to their well-being. A major objective of this book has been to test the major propositions in this critical hypothesis. The data for this test derive from two national surveys conducted in the late 1970s: the 1975–76 Study of Time Use and the 1977 Quality of Employment Survey.

To recall the location of this study in its larger context, one must start with the realization that a major focus of contemporary intellectual feminism has been to develop a theory of the family. More specifically, feminism has attempted to formulate a theory of family inequality. While husbands' physical violence and marital rape have also received attention, a major category of argument within the feminist theory of family inequality concerns the division of family work between husband and wife. In turn, the role overload hypothesis is one of the major lines of argument in feminist social science about the division of family labor, and one which has been reflected in popular thinking about the family as well.

What I formulate as role overload hypothesis is difficult to classify according to the usual typologies of sociological and social psychological theories of the family. Specific propositions within it derive, of course, from other specific theories. For example, economic theories of time allocation, as revised and modified by Geerken and Gove (1983) and Huber and Spitze (1983) now include sex role attitudes. Wives' desire for greater husband help can be interpreted in the context of equity theory (Hatfield and Traupmann, 1980). The set of propositions as a whole, however, draws instead from what can be called feminist theory. Others may contest the view, but I hold that feminist theory has had no less impact on contemporary conceptualizations of the family than has the "new home economics", or other sociological or economic theories. Yet the theoretical contribution of feminism, in this or other areas, is less easily acknowledged because feminism is only beginning to be academically recognized.

The five propositions I have identified as part of the role overload hypothesis provide an organizing structure for the large volume of past research and new analysis presented in the book. My goal has been to explore a variety of issues related to the division of family labor, using these propositions as initial guides to what to observe in the data, and with the expectation that the data may dictate considerable reformulation of key ideas. My approach has been guided by the belief that there is considerable potential in the family for sex inequality, but also by the sense that many common assumptions about the precise nature of this inequality, and the mechanisms by which it operates may need revision. Thus, my objective was not as much to prove these propositions true, as to use them as a guide for inspecting the data to find out what *is* true. They have served well toward this end.

The present chapter develops a broader analysis than was appropriate in the earlier chapters of the sex role issues in husbands' and wives' family roles today. This discussion includes examination of a question not heretofore considered. Though the surveys used in this book could not address it, it is one of the questions most frequently asked about the family by those concerned about sex roles: Is husbands' family participation increasing? As we will see, the answer to this question has important implications for the interpretation of several of the other topics considered in this book.

Before undertaking this discussion, a methodological observation should be made. Using data from *two* national surveys to investigate any issue implies that the results have to pass a rather stringent statistical test to be considered meaningful. Strictly speaking, in order to assert that a phenomenon or relationship exists, it must be statistically significant in both surveys; if it exists in only one, it is technically "unreplicated." A less stringent criterion is that significant results in one survey must be matched by at least nonsignificant trends in the other. Many associations found in one survey fail to meet even the latter, less demanding test. On the other hand, when a relationship is replicated in both surveys, one can have considerable confidence in it.

When there are discrepancies in the findings obtained with the two surveys, one can try to interpret them in light of the methodological differences between the two surveys. There are particularly important differences in the two surveys' measures of time use (time diaries vs. respondents' summary estimates) and in the restrictiveness of their definitions of husbands and wives in one- and two-earner couples. In most cases, however, it is not clear how these methodological variations might contribute to the discrepancies in findings.

However, in one case it is: The results in Chapter 2 about the most fundamental proposition of the sex role perspective, concerning the inequity revealed in husbands' failure to do more when their wives are employed and employed wives' overload. On this critical issue, the two surveys yield quite different results. Here, taking into account the differences in the time use measures in the two surveys leads to an important new interpretation. Our overview of the contemporary issues in husbands' and wives' family roles begins with this question.

HOW INEQUITABLE IS THE DIVISION
OF FAMILY WORK TODAY?

Earlier time use research showed unequivocally that husbands did not, on the average, perform more family work when their wives were employed than when their wives were full-time homemakers. Further, the employed wife had a total work load (family and paid work combined) that was typically considerably higher than her husband's. Both kinds of comparisons indicated serious inequities in the division of family work.

The time use data from the late 1970s analyzed in this book reveal a more complex picture. To recapitulate, in the Study of Time Use, employed wives' role overload relative to their husbands' has all but disappeared; the difference between employed wives' total work and their husband's is only 12 minutes a day. Since the STU's time diary methodology is identical to that used in one of the major earlier surveys which had demonstrated employed wives' overload (Robinson, 1977a), these data clearly show that something about spouses' patterns of time use has changed over the decade between the two surveys. The mitigation of employed wives' role overload in these data, however, does not seem to be due to their husbands doing more in the family when their wives are employed.

The Quality of Employment Survey's measure of family time use, respondents' summary estimates, appears to tap a broader range of activities than do time diaries. According to data from this survey, employed wives continue to be overloaded relative to their husbands, by about 2.2 hours per day. Nonetheless, in these data, husbands of employed wives report performing about half an hour more family work per day than their sole-breadwinner counterparts. Since the time diary data in the STU are more "objective" than the respondent estimates in the QES, it could be argued that the former should be given greater weight.

However, I prefer the interpretation that both surveys' results have validity, but concern somewhat different phenomena. In essence, it was argued earlier that the Study of Time Use assesses family work according to a narrow definition, while the Quality of Employment Survey uses a broader definition. We noted that the disparity between the two surveys' results on husbands' and wives' levels of housework was quite small, while on childcare it was much greater. Childcare in fact represents a continuum of activities ranging from intense, direct interaction to merely being in the same place as the child. The coding of "primary activities" in time diaries assesses the former, narrower form of childcare; while respondents' own estimates include this as well as the broader, more diffuse form. In support of this interpretation, comparison of the QES figures for childcare with data from an earlier time diary study (Robinson, 1977a) concerning "total child contact" (the total amount of time individuals spent with children, of which time coded as childcare interaction was only a small part) indicated a general correspondence between the two. The QES data clearly reflect a broader definition of family work than does the STU.

If so, then these data reveal an important change in the nature of employed wives' role overload during the decade ending in the late 1970s. In the 1960s, employed wives had total work loads substantially higher than their husbands' both when the most narrowly defined family activities are considered, and when the broader array of activities are considered (see data on the latter in Robinson, 1977a) in particular. By the late 1970s, employed wives are still overloaded at the broader level, but are no longer stressed at the narrower level. Employed wives' overload has been mitigated in direct housework and childcare activities, but not in the broader range of these activities that actually constitute the vast majority of all family work.

Another part of our interpretation concerns husbands' responsiveness to wives' employment. Husbands appear to increase their family work at the broader level both in the earlier period (Robinson, 1977a) and the current one (QES). But in neither period do they show an increase at the narrower level.

This is a complex pattern of results, simultaneously involving several different comparisons. To explore what this pattern really means, let us start with one specific contrast: the decline in employed wives' overload in the narrow sense during the decade ending in the late 1970s. To understand this change, we must examine some larger historical trends in husbands' and wives' performance of family work.

CHANGES IN SPOUSES' LEVELS
OF FAMILY WORK IN THE
TWENTIETH CENTURY

Both Newson and Newson (1965) and Lopata (1971: 11) have asserted that men's level of family work is much higher than it was a generation ago, but are able to offer only impressionistic evidence to support this assertion. However, a number of different studies have examined this question empirically. The one investigating the longest time interval is Caplow and Chadwick's (1979, 1982) replication of the "Middletown" study (one of the classic American community studies), using the same midwestern town first studied by Robert and Helen Merrill Lynd in the mid-1920s. The Lynds' 1924 study had asked wives to report how much time they and their husbands spent in household and childcare activities. (The Lynds apparently borrowed these measures from the time use research then being conducted by home economist Martha Van Rensselaer and her colleagues at Cornell.) Caplow and Chadwick found that both fathers and mothers spent more time with their children in 1978 than in 1924. About 10 percent of working class fathers were reported by their wives as spending no time with their children, compared to only 2 percent in 1978 — a change from one father in ten, to one in 50. The percentage of fathers spending more than an hour per day with their children increased significantly from 68 to 77 percent in the same group. (The researchers unfortunately did not break down the "over one hour" category any further.) Figures in the "business class" families were quite parallel.

Sanik (1979, 1981, 1983) compared data from Walker and Woods' (1976) time diary study in Syracuse, N.Y. in 1967–68 with data from a 1977 replication of this study. Specifically, Sanik compared the two-parent, two-child families in the two surveys. In multivariate analyses which controlled for both the husband's and wife's hours in employment, the ages of the two children, and the wife's level of education, fathers' time in all family work increased from 104 to 130 minutes per day, or an increase of 24 minutes. However, Walker and Woods' original study (as well as the 1977 replication) had highly oversampled families with very young children (those aged under two), because of the particular objectives of the study. When Sanik (1981, 1983) weighted the 1977 sample to project the results to a truly representative group of fathers, the increase in fathers' family care was no longer evident. These data suggest that fathers with very young children are spending significantly more time in family roles than they used to, while there has been little or no change in fathers of older children. On the issue of wives' time, Sanik found a decrease from 7.4 to 6.8 hours per day in the weighted analysis.

One of the major ongoing national survey series, the Panel Study of Income Dynamics, has collected respondents' estimates of their time in housework ("cooking, cleaning, and other work around the house") every year, starting in the late 1960s. Both Nickols (1976; Nickols and Metzen, 1982) and Hofferth (1981) found increases in husbands' reports of housework, with other variables controlled, between 1968 and the present. An intensive study with a much smaller sample, Daniels and Weingarten's (1981) study of 86 families in the Boston area, also indicates that fathers' time with young children is increasing. Twice as many children born to men in the study during the 1970s received care on a regular daily basis than children born in the 1950s and 1960s (exact percentages not given).

The single most important source of information about trends in family time use are comparative analyses of time diary data from the 1975–76 Study of Time Use, the 1965–66 Study of Americans' Use of Time, and the 1980–81 Study of Time Use[1], all large-scale national surveys. The several analyses now available report contradictory and puzzling results regarding changes between 1965 and 1976. According to Robinson's analyses of the urban samples in the two surveys, married men's average time in family work increased by 0.7 hours per week, a 6 percent increase over men's 1965–66 baseline of 9.0 hours per week.[2] During the same period, married women's time decreased markedly — about four hours per week for employed wives, and 6.7 hours per week for full-time homemakers, a drop of about 13 percent in both groups. Robinson (1977b: 20) described this decrease in women's time in family work as "unparalleled in historical time use comparisons." Robinson (1980) observed that this decrease occurred during a decade of remarkable diffusion of household technology, but found little support for the hypothesis that increases in this technology accounted for women's decline. Most of the decline in family work occurred in routine cleaning and maintenance activities. There was as well, however, a small decline in time with children, even after correction to a per-child basis (i.e., taking into account smaller family size).[3]

Robinson (1980) further notes that the 1975–76 sample differs from the earlier one on a variety of characteristics that are potentially related to levels of family work. For example, in the 1975 sample wives were more likely to be employed and men were more likely to be married; both were more likely to have smaller families, more education, and live in rented housing. When these differences between the two samples were taken into account, Robinson found that men in 1975–76 actually spent about 5 percent less time in family work than did men in the 1965–66 sample. Controlling for the same factors narrows the estimate for women's decline in family work from 17 percent to 7 percent.

These results are worth thoughtful but critical discussion. First, it is puzzling that controlling for the same demographic factors decreases the estimate for men's family work but increases the estimate for women's. For example, if families have fewer children in the later time period, statistical control for this factor should increase the estimate of *both* parents' time in the later period. In reality, of the three major demographic factors Robinson identifies as narrowing the estimate for women's family work from 17 to 7 percent, wives' employment is not related to men's family work in these data, and the distributions on presence and ages of children actually differ little between the two samples. Perhaps the demographic factor transforming men's raw increase of 6 percent to a statistically adjusted decrease of 5 percent is the lower rate of labor force participation of men in 1975 than in 1965 (Deuterman, 1977). Robinson does not provide enough detailed information on the analysis in the male sample to determine whether this is the case. If so, the conventional interpretation would be that when rates of labor force participation are controlled for, men did slightly less family work in 1975 than in 1965. But a more substantively meaningful interpretation would be that between 1965 and 1975 men shifted simultaneously toward both lower labor force participation and higher participation in family work.

It should also be observed that even if the results of Robinson's revised analysis are accepted, they do not mean that husbands did not perform more family work on the average in 1975 than in 1965; they actually did. Rather, these results mean that the observed average increase in men's family time is due to a higher proportion of husbands in 1975 than in 1965 having characteristics associated with high participation in family work, rather than to a simple temporal trend for all subgroups of fathers to participate more.

The interpretation of Robinson's results is further complicated by the fact that other analyses of the same data yield somewhat different results. For example, Duncan and Stafford (1980) report a comparison of persons employed 10 or more hours per week in the same two surveys, finding no overall difference between married males in any of four family work subcategories. In earlier analyses, however, these investigators reported that married men's family work time increased by 1.5 hours per week (Stafford and Duncan, 1978; Hill and Stafford, 1980). None of these analyses appear to control on parental status, the age of the youngest child, or the number of children — potentially fatal flaws in this kind of analysis. Juster (in press: Table 11.2) provides yet another and slightly different set of figures for men and women in 1965 and 1975. Juster's analysis indicates that the family time of men aged 25–44 decreased by 3.3 hours per week, while men aged 45–64 showed a 2.8 hour a week increase.

Fortunately, however, Juster (in press, especially Figure 11.3) also provides results from the newer 1980–81 national time diary survey. The 1980–81 sample consisted of those in the 1975–76 study who could be located and who agreed to be interviewed again; strictly speaking it is not representative of the 1981 population. Nonetheless, a comparison of family time use between 1965 and 1981 yields important results. In these data, younger men's (25–44 in each survey) time in family work increased 2.3 more hours per week (19.5 percent more than they did in 1965), while older men's (45–64) also increased 2.3 hours (20.5 percent more). A reasonable interpretation of these data taken together is that there is a long-term trend toward increased male participation. Even if the 1965–75 comparison unambiguously indicated a male decrease, it would only be a short-term downward "blip" in a longer-term upward trend. Juster's data also show younger women decreasing their family time by 14.1 hours per week (a decrease of 30.7 percent) between 1965 and 1981, while older women have decreased theirs by 7.6 hours per week (21.2 percent).

When smaller family size is taken into account, it is clear that the average child of a given age is spending more minutes per day with his or her father in 1981 than in 1965. Men are also performing a higher proportion of the couple's total family work. In Juster's (in press) data, both younger men's and older men's family work as a proportion of the total for both sexes rose from about 20 percent to a little over 30 percent between 1965 and 1981 — a rather substantial move toward the 50 percent that would signify equality.

Analyses of possible changes in the composition (as opposed to the absolute level) of men's family work have not yet been reported in detail for these national time diary data. However, Duncan et al. (1973) examined such compositional changes in a study of trends in the proportional division of labor between husband and wife between 1955 and 1971. Duncan et al. administered a 1971 sample of Detroit wives six of the eight items Blood and Wolfe had first used in a similarly drawn sample of Detroit wives 16 years earlier. Duncan et al.'s comparison of their results with Blood and Wolfe's 1955 data revealed some changes, but the pattern was mixed. For example, wives reported that their husbands got their own breakfast somewhat more often, but did the evening dishes less often. There seemed to be no clear trend toward either greater or less husband participation in housework, or for either greater sharing or greater specialization of family work between husband and wife.

Overall, the preponderance of evidence is that men's time in the family is increasing while women's is decreasing. Men and women are moving toward convergence in their family time, though it will clearly be a long time — if ever — before they reach parity. More of the convergence is due to women's decrease than to men's increase, though men's increase is not trivial. This might be interpreted as revealing greater male resistance to sex role convergence. Yet it should be recalled that though the increase in men's time may be small, it is occurring amidst more general social trends that decrease adults' time in childcare and housework. Women's decreasing time in the family is congruent with the long-term trend toward fewer children (which depresses both childcare and housework time, since children generate much of the need for housework). Men's increasing family time goes against this trend.

WHY ROLE OVERLOAD, IN THE
NARROW SENSE, DISAPPEARED

The disappearance of employed wives' narrowly defined role overload compared to their husbands is quite consistent with these trends over time. Superimposing these trends on the patterns of marital time use observed in the mid-1960s leads precisely to the new configuration evident in the 1975-76 STU data. There are four groups to consider: employed wives, full-time homemakers, husbands of employed wives, and husbands of nonemployed wives. In the mid-1960s data (see Table 2.1), employed wives stood out from the other three groups as distinctively high in their total work load; the two groups of husbands were considerably lower, and housewives slightly lower than either group of husbands. Since then, wives as a group have decreased their family work, narrowly defined, and husbands have increased theirs. As a result, employed wives' total work load has been brought in line with that of both husband groups. This occurred even without the possible additional phenomenon of husbands increasing their family work specifically in response to their wives' employment. Thus, the old pattern in which employed wives were uniquely high in total work compared to all other groups has been transformed into a new configuration in which non-employed wives now stand out as uniquely low in their total work.

The three groups that have both a paid work role and a family role (sole-earner husbands, dual-earner husbands, and employed wives) clearly hold these two roles in different relative proportions. But these three groups appear to share in common a higher total work load than those who hold a role in only one domain (nonemployed wives). None of these three groups, of course, appears to have an average total work load as high in absolute terms of that of employed wives in the mid-1960s. This is indicated both in Robinson's (1977b) analysis of 1965-75 as well as Juster's (in press) examination of 1965–81.

In essence, the trends toward convergence of husbands' and wives' overall levels of family time have led to a more specific convergence in the total work loads of husbands and wives within two-earner couples. Thus, the narrowly defined role overload so evident in the time use studies of the 1960s has been mitigated. Whatever the source of these changes in family work patterns, they have led to an entirely new realignment of marital subgroups in terms of their total work load.

DO HUSBANDS DO MORE WHEN THEIR WIVES ARE EMPLOYED?

The conceptual relationship between (1) husbands' responsiveness to wives' employment and (2) employed wives' overload has shifted throughout this book. Initially, the issue of husbands' responsiveness was the more theoretically central of the two because it provides a critical test of resource theory. In this context, role overload is conceptualized as a side effect of husbands' not increasing their family time when their wives are employed. In the role overload hypothesis, the relationship between the two issues is reversed. In this perspective, role overload is the more theoretically salient phenomenon because it is such a direct manifestation of marital inequality. The lack of husbands' responsiveness is viewed as the specific mechanism leading to this inequality.

Consistent with this changed emphasis, the discussion so far has focussed primarily on overload. Nonetheless, there are some further interpretive points to make about the degree of husbands' responsiveness to wives' employment. Our two surveys provide discrepant results on this point. On the basis of data in both the QES and Robinson's (1977a) data on "total child contact" in 1965–66, I argue that husbands whose wives are employed do not increase their family work in the narrow sense, but do show an increase in the broader forms of family participation.

Chapter 2's review of past research on the responsiveness of husbands to wives' employment focussed on Blood and Wolfe's (1960) proportional approach and on the major time diary studies. Many other studies, of course, have investigated this effect. Most of these have used Blood and Wolfe's measure (see Bahr, 1974; also Gecas, 1976; Slocum and Nye, 1976; Duncan and Duncan, 1978; Perrucci et al., 1978). Other studies using less sophisticated absolute measures of family work also find an increase (Nolan, 1963; Young and Willmott, 1973; Piotrowski, 1971; Safilios-Rothschild, 1970). These studies suffer from one or more of several defects: not using or reporting significance tests, using extremely global or vague single-item measures (e.g., "does your husband ever help you in the house?").

Some large-sample analyses using absolute measures remain, however, which find large and significant increments in husbands' family work when wives are employed. These studies assess, I believe, changes in husbands' family role at the broader level. Two of these are analyses of data from the Panel Study of Income Dynamics, cited earlier in another context. In Farkas' (1976) analysis of 1967–72 data, husbands reported spending nearly twice as many hours in housework if their wives were employed at all during 1967. Hofferth (1981: 9), analyzing 1968–1976 PSID data, also found a small relationship between wives' hours of employment and husbands' housework.[4]

In a 1974 national survey concerning parenthood, Hoffman (1978) asked wives: "Has your husband ever helped you with the housework? (If yes) These days, does he help regularly, occasionally, or only rarely?" Hoffman reports data for this item for wives with either no or one child, by wife's education and degree of employment (distinguishing full-time from part-time). In all groups, employed wives reported their husbands doing more housework and childcare. Interestingly, in both the high and low education groups, wives with one child reported less husband help with housework than wives with no children.

To briefly note a number of more recent studies, Kamerman (1980), Model (1981), and Bohen and Viveros-Long (1981), all using what appear to be broad measures, find an increase in husbands. Owen, Chase-Lansdale, and Lamb (1981) and Russell (1982) do not, though the latter finds that husbands of employed wives spend more time with sole responsibility for their children. Studies making this comparison are appearing with increasing frequency.

In what is apparently the only intensive longitudinal study, Presser (1977) examined the housework and childcare tasks performed by husbands of wives who were not employed in 1973 but were employed in 1976, in a larger sample of 210 mothers in three New York City boroughs. In this intriguing analysis, Presser found that 44 percent of the fathers increased the number of household tasks they did, 45 percent performed the same number of tasks, and 11 percent actually reduced their tasks.

Though this is a complex literature to integrate, certain patterns are evident. At the narrow level, the STU and the preponderance of other available data suggests that husbands increase their absolute level of family work little, if at all, when wives are employed. A few studies suggest, though, that there might be a significant increase in this narrow level of family work among fathers of very young children.

At the broader level, studies like the QES, Robinson's (1977b) "total child contact" analyses, and many others suggest that husbands do increase their time in the broader, more diffuse categories of family work. Even though husbands of employed wives do more, the increase is small in absolute magnitude, and employed wives continue to do the bulk of the family work. Finally, at both the narrow and broad levels, husbands' proportion of the couple's total family work increases. Husbands of employed wives clearly perform a higher proportion of the couple's total family work than do sole-breadwinning husbands. In the STU's narrow-level measure, wife-employed husbands did about 32 percent of the couple's total, while sole-breadwinners did 21 percent. In the QES's broader measure, husbands of employed wives perform about 35 percent of their couple's total. This proportional shift is meaningful, and its importance should not be minimized.

Our earlier analysis of how husbands' family time, in the narrow sense, is increasing and wives' is decreasing brings out an overlooked dimension of husbands' responsiveness to their wives' employment. Rather than interpret the similarity in family time use between husbands and wives in the 1975–76 STU as showing that husbands of employed wives do not do more when their wives are employed, one could reasonably argue that husbands of working wives actually are spending more time in the family now than in the past. But this has not been easily evident because sole-breadwinning husbands have increased their family participation as well. In other words, perhaps the question should not be why wife-employed husbands are still so unresponsive to the needs of their wives by not contributing more time when their wives are employed. Rather, the question should be why not only the two-earner husbands, but the sole-breadwinners as well, have increased their family involvement, even though this leads to the latter group increasing their workload relative to their wives'.

It appears that there has been a value shift in our culture toward greater family involvement by husbands. Though clearly related to a similar cultural value change supporting wives' employment, this shift has nonetheless had effects even on those husbands whose wives are *not* employed. What may be happening today is that wives' rising rates of employment have stimulated a change in social values about fatherhood which has brought about an increase in paternal involvement among *all* groups of fathers — both fathers whose wives are employed and fathers whose wives are not.

THE CHANGING NATURE OF ROLE OVERLOAD

It should be emphasized that the diminution of employed wives' narrowly defined role overload does not mean that all the problems of the employed wife have been solved. First, role overload continues for employed wives at the broader level of family work, conceptualized as including a broader range of childcare and housework responsibilities. Employed wives' overload has been mitigated in the narrow sense, but not in the broader sense. Just because the form of overload remaining contains more diffuse activities does not mean that its effects are any less serious. In fact, our data provides direct evidence that wives feel dissatisfied with their husbands' contribution when it is low in this broader area, according to husbands' reports of both.

Second, while employed wives and employed husbands may work the same number of total hours at the narrow level, the relative balance of paid work and family time within that total is clearly different. In the STU, about 45 percent of employed wives' total time is spent in the family, compared to about 21 percent of dual-earner husbands' time. These different proportions of paid work and family time can have important consequences.

These data indicate that employed wives will not be overloaded compared to their husbands *if* they have the extent of involvement in paid work that is currently typical of the vast majority of employed wives, i.e., one that is considerably less substantial than their husbands' in terms of both the average number of hours worked per week as well as continuity over time. Insofar as increases in earnings and level of job responsibility are contingent on being able to put in long hours on a continuous basis through adulthood, employed wives' current patterns of paid work and family roles obviously leave employed wives at a disadvantage compared to their husbands. Particularly important is economic insecurity in later life when husbands are gone, and pension rights resulting from husbands's employment are inadequate or nonexistent.

By analogy, there may be negative consequences for husbands of another kind. Research suggests that aging fathers who live alone receive less contact and social support from their adult children than do aging mothers (Stueve, O'Donnell, and Lein, 1980). Perhaps the investment that fathers make in the family earlier in life is insufficient to lead their children to want to be in contact with them later on. Underinvesting in either the paid work *or* family sphere may cause difficulties in the later years.

More broadly, there has been a historical evolution in the nature of the most salient problem faced by employed wives. In the not so distant past, the primary problem was that husbands did not want their wives to work at all (Erksine, 1971). This attitude then weakened, as husbands came to see wives' employment as permissible, even desirable, as long as wives continued to perform all their traditional family roles. This attitude shift did not mean that employed wives no longer had any difficulties. Rather, the problem changed from being primarily one of outright and direct husband resistance to his wife's being employed, to being primarily an issue of role overload, both in the narrow and broad sense.

Now, in turn, the problem of role overload in the narrow sense has been greatly reduced, at least for the average employed wife. Once again, this change does not mean that the employed wife's difficulties have disappeared. Rather, it means that the difficulties faced by employed wives now take two forms: (1) the role overload that remains at the broader level of family work; and (2) low occupational and earnings mobility if they want to avoid overload by limiting their hours or continuity in the paid labor market. In the past all employed wives, on the average, experienced considerable role overload, narrowly defined. Now they are overloaded in the narrow sense only if they want to have the same chances for occupational advancement and earnings as men, by working full-time and continuously through adulthood.

This study also contributes to the understanding of how a high level of time in family and paid work has negative consequences in marital relationships. The discrepancy between a husband's and wife's levels of total work described here as wives' overload appears to decrease family adjustment primarily by virtue of the husband's performance being so low rather than the wife's performance being so high. Stated another way, there appears to be good evidence for an "inequity" effect, but not much evidence for the more intuitively expected "exhaustion" effect. Perhaps in the past, when narrowly defined overload was more evident and overall levels of total work were somewhat higher for all marital groups than they are now, the exhaustion effect may have occurred. To sum up: In the past role overload in the narrow sense was paramount, and perhaps had an impact via an exhaustion effect. More recently, role overload is apparent only in the broader sense, and influences employed wives' well-being primarily via an inequity effect.

SOCIAL ATTITUDES ABOUT THE
DIVISION OF FAMILY WORK

Another central focus of this book is social attitudes about the division of family work. Our data suggest that sex role ideology, in the narrow sense in which it is usually conceptualized and assessed, does not seem vitally connected to issues of family work. Perhaps "consciousness-raising" is not adequately reflected by scores on attitude items with five-point response scales! On the other hand, the data demonstrate that a wife's wishing her own specific husband would perform more housework and childcare is extremely important in its effects. There are some important leads for future research in our findings. For instance, in the STU, non-employed wives more often than employed wives say they want help with childcare. As another example, one subgroup of wives appear to want their husbands to do more childcare to respond to wives' needs. Another subgroup, however, appears to want their husbands to do more not to help their wives, but for their children's and their own sake.

Employed wives' own reports and husbands' perceptions of their wives' desires for greater participation on the survey questions in the QES give somewhat different estimates of the proportion of wives wanting a change. In employed wives' reports, 36 percent want more housework and 42 percent want more childcare. By contrast, the percentage of dual-earner husbands believing their wives want them to do more are 55 and 57 percent. Whose reports are accepted determines whether the conclusion is only that (1) a substantial minority or (2) a bare majority of employed wives want more contribution from their husbands. In this instance, there are no clear grounds on which to give one set of reports more credence than the other.

In either case, it is perhaps surprising that so many employed wives appear content with their husbands' level of family participation. The belief that housework and childcare are ultimately the wife's responsibility (no matter what her employment status) is widely and deeply held. In addition, some wives may not want their husbands to do more because they feel that the home domain is their territory, and they derive a sense of psychological identity from this role.

Some commentators (Robinson, 1977a) have stressed that the rate of increase in wives' wishes for enlarged family role in their husbands is quite slow. Comparison of our data with Robinson's suggest that this increase will continue in the future if only because employed wives will become a larger proportion of all wives, and employed wives more often want their husbands to do more. Although an employed wife's desire for greater husband participation does vary with her husband's level of performance, it is noteworthy that within both employed and non-employed wives, desires for greater husband contribution have remained at the same level even as husbands' actual average family participation has in fact increased — a clear example of a revolution of rising expectations. More is being expected from men than used to be the case. Thus, wives' desires reflect in part a more general value shift in the culture about the appropriateness and desirability of greater husband participation. In fact, changes in husbands' actual family behavior and wives' desire for their greater participation may be reflections of the same underlying shift in beliefs.

HUSBANDS AND THEIR FAMILY ROLE

By some criteria, these data show considerable evidence of change in husbands. A variety of studies demonstrates increases in husbands' average amount of time spent in family roles. This absolute increase is occurring in spite of the fact that the historical decline in family size exerts pressure in the other direction, and is in fact having this effect on women to a strong degree. In Juster's (in press) comparison of 1965 and 1981, husbands' average proportion of the couple's total family work rose from about 20 percent to about 30 percent. In our two surveys, dual-earner husbands perform about 30 to 35 percent of the couple's total family work, compared to sole-breadwinning husbands' 20 percent. In these same data, high levels of total work and family work in husbands are associated with positive family adjustment and overall well-being. Altogether, these results augur well for future enlargement of husbands' family role.

Nonetheless, a fundamental question remains: Why do husbands currently do so much less than wives? It is clear that the demands of the work role by themselves are not a sufficient explanation. In the present study's data, time in paid work exerts some negative influence on time in the family. But a large difference between husbands and wives in levels of family work is evident even when work hours are controlled for. It should also be stressed that the effect of paid work hours on husbands' family time was much stronger for housework than for childcare; in fact, in the STU, work hours had no effect on childcare at all.

The work role is only one of many possible social explanations for husbands' low family time relative to wives. Others include: modelling after one's own father; social attitudes; lack of support from wives or peers; lack of specific skills. Most of these factors are probably important for at least some men. Taking each into account, one at a time, a substantial sex difference still remains. Presumably, a truly complete list of factors taken together would account for all the sex differences. These factors taken together comprise the environmental/socialization explanation of men's low family time.

But in the minds of many, a deeper question remains: even if all the variance in men's family work time could be explained through a combination of these social factors, is not the real source of men's low participation that men simply do not want to do it? Could not all the simpler explanatory factors be seen as a system for men reinforcing themselves for not wanting to do it? At a deeper level, the question really being asked is whether men are or are not morally responsible for their low family participation. Does this low participation occur because of factors which men are really not responsible for, or do men bear an ultimate responsibility for it?

This question is ultimately a moral one, and cannot be answered through a purely scientific analysis. I believe that rather than devote effort to debating this question, it is more important to identify and investigate the major social processes which contribute to husbands' low family participation. The following seem to be the major facilitating factors[5]:

(1) Motivation: Husbands have to want to participate. Many different factors influence husbands' degree of motivation, including the husband's experience in his family of origin, attitudes of wives and peers, media images, mid-life reevaluations, etc.

(2) Supports: It helps a husband to feel that others (one's wife, relatives, male peers) favor his participation and give positive reinforcement for it. These significant others also provide advice and concrete help in the performance of the family role, which helps make the role self-reinforcing.

(3) Skills: Husbands have to know how to perform family and child-rearing tasks. Some men are motivated to participate more and would receive social supports for greater participation, but feel they don't know what to do and how to act. Having specific family skills makes participation a more self-reinforcing, satisfying experience for the husband, and gives him more self-confidence in this role.

(4) Absence of structural barriers: Some men develop motivation for greater family involvement, find supports, and develop skills, but then feel constrained by institutional barriers. Inflexible or otherwise highly demanding job schedules are particularly important. But also significant are the timing of career demands for those husbands who have careers. The greatest effort is required at the early stages of career development, when the demands of the family role are also at their peak. In that vast majority of families in which the husband's wage is higher than the wife's, there is also a trade-off between men's family participation and total family income. The husband doing more in the family ostensibly in theory frees the wife to put more time in paid work to earn more. But since her wage is typically much lower than her husband's, such a choice reduces family income. The husband-wife wage ratio can act as a powerful structural disincentive to husbands' participation.[6]

These four factors differ greatly in the social institutions through which they operate, and in the ease with which they can be altered. The fact that family participation and family satisfaction have positive correlates for husbands' well-being, and that men's psychological involvement in the family is so high, provide a positive context in which changes in these factors can lead to an increase in men's family participation.

At the same time, it must be recognized that increased family participation may impose costs for men as well. A high number of hours in family work by husbands predicts family adjustment, but high hours in paid work predicts another positive outcome, overall well-being. Just as for women, integrating paid work and family roles present profound issues of choice for men, choices within men themselves as well as in the minds of those who judge them. There is no getting around the fact that men who participate more directly in their families must be, on the average, less productive and ambitious in their paid work.

Certainly, every effort should be made to reduce the unnecessary conflict between the two roles created by arbitrary and rigid institutional practices, particularly concerning work scheduling and parental leave. Further implementation and development of innovative policies and practices in these areas will do much to mitigate the conflicts that many experience now. But rearranging the pattern of paid work time, without reducing its overall extent, can go only so far to free men in their family role. Ultimately, increasing men's family role means reducing their paid work time. This entails potentially heavy costs for men and for their families (since men's wages are higher), particularly during a time of slow growth in workers' wages and productivity. Families often consciously recognize these costs (Lein, 1979).

There may be a few "supermen" who, like the equally small minority of "superwomen", are able to combine extraordinarily high levels of involvement in both roles. But these minorities are inappropriate as models for the large majority of average men and women. Probably the more typical pattern is reflected in Bailyn's (1974, 1977) finding in a professional-technical sample that men who are highly involved in their families, and accommodate their work role to it, are less ambitious in their occupation. If they work in a highly demanding career line, they devalue themselves for it.

While reforms and innovations will help, there is an unavoidable nexus of both genuine conflict and authentic choice between work and family that men, women, and society as a whole must honestly face. No one wishes a self-serving abdication of the breadwinner role on men's part. But it is clear that the realignment of work and family roles between the sexes and within each sex now underway in our society, and specifically the enlargement of men's family role, means that we must accept a considerable decrease in men's current breadwinner responsibility, and a sharing of this responsibility with women going far beyond current social attitudes.

NOTES

1. Analyses of the 1980–81 survey (Juster and Stafford, in press) do not appear to examine the relationship between wives' employment status and either husbands' family time or wives' overload.

2. Robinson (1977b) reports a value for husbands' "family care" (evidently the sum of housework and childcare) for 1965–66 which is not consistent with data given in his earlier (1977a) volume, particularly its Table 3.6 (giving 11.3 hours per week). Apparently, certain activity categories were excluded from family care in the later report.

3. These observations revise Robinson's (1977b) earlier statements that "few major breakthroughs in labor-saving technology had diffused widely through society" in this period, and that women's childcare time had *increased* on a per-child basis.

4. However, Nickols and Metzen (1982), using the same data, did not find this effect in a somewhat different comparison, the effect of wives' hours of employment in a given year on husbands' housework hours the following year. They found that the wife's time allocation to paid work outside the home had little to do with the time the husbands allocated to work in the home a year later. Nickols and Metzen also noted that the pattern of time allocation by each spouse tended to persist from one year to the next.

5. The formulation of these factors was developed jointly with Michael E. Lamb and James A. Levine.

6. Of the available studies directly examining the influence of the husband-wife wage ratio or husband's wage on the division of family work, Farkas (1976) finds no effect, while Model (1981) does.

Bibliography

ADAMEK, R. and W. GOUDY (1966) "Identification, sex, and change in college major." Sociology of Education 39, 2: 183–199.

ANDRE, R. (1981) Homemakers: The Forgotten Workers. Chicago: University of Chicago Press.

ANDREWS, F. and WITHEY, S. (1976) Social Indicators of Well-Being. New York: Plenum.

BAHR, S. (1974) "Effects on power and division of labor," pp. 167–185 in L.W. Hoffman and F.I. Nye (eds.) Working Mothers. San Francisco: Jossey-Bass.

BAILYN, L. (1970) "Career and family orientations of husbands and wives in relation to marital happiness." Human Relations 23 (June): 97–113.

——— (1974) "Accommodation as career strategy: Implications for the realm of work." Working Paper 728–74, Sloan School of Management, Massachusetts Institute of Technology.

——— (1977) "Involvement and accommodation in technical careers: An inquiry into the relation to work at mid-career," pp. 109–132 in J. Van Maanen (ed.) Organizational Careers: Some New Perspectives. London: Wiley International.

BARNETT, R. and G.K. BARUCH (1979) Multiple Roles and Well-Being: A Study of Mothers of Preschool Age Children. Wellesley, MA: Wellesley College Center for Research on Women.

BECKER, G. (1976) The Economic Approach to Human Behavior. Chicago: University of Chicago Press.

BECKMAN, L.J. and B.B. HOUSER (1979) "The more you have, the more you do: The relationships between wife's employment, sex-role attitudes and household behavior." Psychology of Women Quarterly 4 (Winter): 160–174.

BERK, R.A. (1980) "The new home economics: An agenda for sociological research," pp. 113–148 in S.F. Berk (ed.) Women and Household Labor. Beverly Hills, CA: Sage.

——— and BERK, S.F. (1979) Labor and Leisure at Home: Consent and Organization of the Household Day. Beverly Hills, CA: Sage.

BERK, S.F. (1979) "Husbands at home: Organization of the husband's household day," pp. 125–158 in K.F. Weinstein (ed.) Working Women and Families. Beverly Hills, CA: Sage.

——— and A. SHIH (1980) "Contributions to household labor: Comparing wives' and husbands' reports," pp. 191–228 in S.F. Berk (ed.) Women and Household Labor. Beverly Hills, CA: Sage.

BERNARD, J. (1972) The Future of Marriage. New York: World.

BEST, F. (1981) "Changing sex roles and worklife flexibility." Psychology of Women Quarterly 6:55–71.

BLOOD, R.O. and R. HAMBLIN (1958) "The effect of wife's employment on the family power structure." Social Forces 38 (November): 347–352.

——— and D.M. WOLFE (1960) Husbands and Wives. Glencoe, IL: Free Press.

BOHEN, H. and A. VIVEROS-LONG (1981) Balancing Jobs and Family Life: Do Flexible Work Schedules Help? Philadelphia: Temple University Press.

BOOTH, A. (1977) "Wife's employment and husband's stress: A replication and refutation." Journal of Marriage and the Family 39 (November): 645–650.

——— (1979) "Does wives' employment cause stress for husbands?" Family Coordinator 28 (October): 445–450.

BOWLING, M. (1977) "Sex role attitudes and the division of household labor." Paper presented at the American Sociological Association, Chicago.

BUREAU OF LABOR STATISTICS, U.S. DEPARTMENT OF LABOR (1984) "Current labor statistics." Monthly Labor Review 107 (August): 51–72.

BURKE, R. and T. WEIR (1976) "Relationship of wives' employment status to husband, wife and pair satisfaction and performance." Journal of Marriage and the Family 38 (May): 279–287.

——— and R. DuWORS (1979) "Type A behavior of administrators and wives' reports of marital satisfaction and well-being." Journal of Applied Psychology 64, 1: 57–65.

CAMPBELL, A., P. CONVERSE, and W. RODGERS (1976) The Quality of American Life. New York: Russell Sage.

CAPLOW, T. and B. CHADWICK (1979) "Inequality and life-styles in Middletown, 1920–1978." Social Science Quarterly 60, 3: 367–390.

——— H. BAHR, B. CHADWICK, R. HILL, and M.H. WILLIAMSON (1982) Middletown Families: Fifty Years of Change and Continuity. Minneapolis: University of Minnesota.

CLARK, R. and V. GECAS (1977) "The employed father in America: A role competition analysis." Paper presented at the Pacific Sociological Association.

——— F.I. NYE, and V. GECAS (1978) "Husbands' work involvement and marital role performance." Journal of Marriage and the Family 41 (February): 9–21.

CLEARY, P. and D. MECHANIC (1983) "Sex differences in psychological distress among married people." Journal of Health and Social Behavior 24 (June): 111–121.

DANIELS, P. and K. WEINGARTEN (1981) Sooner or Later: The Timing of Parenthood and Adult Lives. New York: Norton.

DEUTERMAN, W. (1977) "Another look at working-age men who are not in the labor force." Monthly Labor Review 100 (June): 9–14.

DUBIN, R. (1956) "Industrial workers' worlds: A study of the 'central life interests' of industrial workers." Social Problems 3, 1: 53–72.

——— A. HEDLEY, and R. TAVEGGIA (1976) "Attachment to work," in R. Dubin (ed.) Handbook of Work, Organization, and Society. Chicago: Rand McNally.

DUNCAN, G. and F. STAFFORD (1980) "The use of time and technology by households in the United States," in R.G. Ehrenberg (ed.) Research in Labor Economics, vol. 3. Greenwich, CT: JAI Press.

DUNCAN, O., H. SCHUMAN, and B. DUNCAN (1973) Social Change in a Metropolitan Community. New York: Russell Sage.

——— and B. DUNCAN (1978) Sex Typing and Social Roles: A Research Report. New York: Academic.

EISENSTEIN. Z., (ed.) (1979) Capitalist Patriarchy and the Case for Socialist Feminism. New York: Monthly Review Press.

ERICKSEN, J., W. YANCEY, and E. ERICKSEN (1979) "The division of family roles." Journal of Marriage and the Family 41 (May): 301–312.

ERSKINE, H. (1971) "The polls: Women's roles." Public Opinion Quarterly 35, 2: 275–298.

——— (1973) "The polls: Hopes, fears, and regrets." Public Opinion Quarterly 37, 1: 132–145.

FARKAS, G. (1976) "Education, wage rates, and the division of labor between husband and wife." Journal of Marriage and the Family 38 (August): 473–484.

FARRELL, M. and S. ROSENBERG (1982) Men at Midlife. Boston: Auburn House.
FARRELL, W. (1974) The Liberated Man. New York: Random House.
GAVRON, H. (1966) The Captive Housewife. Harmondsworth: Penguin.
GECAS, V. (1976) "The socialization and child care roles," pp. 33–60 in F.I. Nye (ed.) Role Structure and Analysis of the Family. Beverly Hills, CA: Sage.
GEERKEN, M. and W.R. GOVE (1983) At Home and At Work: The Family's Allocation of Labor. Beverly Hills, CA: Sage.
GLAZER, N. (1976) "Housework." Signs: Journal of Women in Culture and Society 1 (Summer): 905–922.
GOVE, W.R. (1972) "The relationship between sex roles, mental illness, and marital status." Social Forces 51 (Spring): 34–44.
——— (1979) "Sex differences in the epidemiology of mental disorder: Evidence and explanations," pp. 23–68 in E. Gomberg and V. Franks (eds.) Gender and Disordered Behavior. New York: Brunner/Mazel.
GRONSETH, E. (1971) "The husband-provider role: A critical appraisal," pp. 11–31 in A. Michel (ed.) Family Issues of Employed Women in Europe and America. Leiden: E.J. Brill.
GROSS, R.H. and R.D. ARVEY (1977) "Marital satisfaction, job satisfaction, and task distribution in the homemaker job." Journal of Vocational Behavior 11 (April): 1–13.
GURIN, G., J. VEROFF, and S. FELD (1960) Americans View Their Mental Health. New York: Basic.
HARRIS, L. and Associates (1971) The Harris Survey Yearbook of Public Opinion 1970. New York: Louis Harris.
HARRY, J. (1976) "Evolving sources of happiness for men over the life cycle: A structural analysis." Journal of Marriage and the Family 38, 2: 289–298.
HARTMANN, H.I. (1981) "The family as the locus of gender, class, and political struggle: The example of housework." Signs: Journal of Women in Culture and Society 6: 366–394.
HATFIELD, E. and J. TRAUPMANN (1980) "Equity and intimacy over the lifespan," in S. Duck and R. Gilmour (eds.) Personal Relationships. London: Academic Press.
HAUENSTEIN, L., S. KASL, and E. HARBURG (1977) "Work status, work satisfaction, and blood pressure among married black and white women." Psychology of Women Quarterly 1 (Summer): 334–350.
HAYGHE, H. (1982) "Marital and family patterns of workers: An update." Monthly Labor Review 105 (May): 53–56.
HERRIN, D. (1983) "Use of time by married couples in multiple roles." Dissertation Abstracts International 44 (July): 01A. (University Microfilms No. 83-13059)
HESSELBART, S. (1976) "Does charity begin at home? Attitudes toward women, household tasks, and household decision-making." Paper presented to the American Sociological Association.
——— (1978) "Some underemphasized issues about men, women, and work." Paper presented to the American Sociological Association, San Francisco.
HILL, C.R., and F. STAFFORD (1980) "Parental care of children: Time diary estimates of quantity, predictability, and variety." Journal of Human Resources 15, 2:218–239.
HOFFERTH, S. (1981) Effects of Number and Timing of Births on Family Well-Being Over the Life Cycle. Washington: Urban Institute.
HOFFMAN, L.W. (1963) "Parental power relations and the division of household tasks," pp. 215–230 in F.I. Nye and L.W. Hofman (eds.) The Employed Mother in America. Chicago: Rand McNally.

———— (1977) "Changes in family roles, socialization, and sex differences." American Psychologist 32 (August): 644–657.

———— (1978) "The effect of the first child on the woman's roles," pp. 340–367 in W.B. Miller and L.F. Newman (eds.) The First Child and Family Formation. Chapel Hill, NC: Carolina Population Center, University of North Carolina.

HOOD, J. (1983) Becoming a Two-Job Family. New York: Praeger.

HOUSE, J. (1979) Occupational Stress and the Mental and Physical Health of Factory Workers. Ann Arbor, MI: Institute for Social Research.

HUBER, J. and G. SPITZE (1983) Sex Stratification: Children, Housework, and Jobs. New York: Academic Press.

HUNT, M. (1976) "Today's man: Redbook's exclusive Gallup survey on the emerging male." Redbook (October): 112ff.

INSTITUTE OF LIFE INSURANCE (1974) Youth 1974: Finance Related Attitudes. New York: Institute of Life Insurance Research Services.

JUSTER, F.T. (in press) "A note on recent changes in time use," pp. 397–422 in F.T. Juster and F. Stafford (eds.) Studies in the Measurement of Time Allocation. Ann Arbor, MI: Institute for Social Research.

———— P. COURANT, G. DUNCAN, J. ROBINSON, and F. STAFFORD (1978) Time Use in Economic and Social Accounts — Codebook. Ann Arbor, MI: Inter-University Consortium for Political and Social Research.

———— and F. STAFFORD [eds.] (in press) Studies in the Measurement of Time Allocation. Ann Arbor, MI: Institute for Social Research.

KAMERMAN, S.B. (1980) Parenting in an Unresponsive Society. New York: Free Press.

KESSLER, R. and J. McRAE (1982) "The effect of wives' employment on the mental health of married men and women." Journal of Health and Social Behavior 47 (April): 216–227.

LaROCCO, J., J. HOUSE, and J. FRENCH (1980) "Social support, occupational stress, and health." Journal of Health and Social Behavior 21 (September) 202–218.

LaROSSA, R. (1977) Conflict and Power in Marriage: Expecting the First Child. Beverly Hills, CA: Sage.

LEIN, L. (1979) "Male participation in the home: Impact of social supports and breadwinners responsibility on the allocation of tasks." Family Coordinator 28, 3: 489–496.

————, M. DURHAM, M. PRATT, M. SCHUDSON, R. THOMAS, and H. WEISS (1974) Final Report: Work and Family Life. Cambridge, MA: Center for the Study of Public Policy.

———— (1983) Families Without Villains. Lexington, MA: Lexington Books.

LOPATA, H. (1971) Occupation: Housewife. New York: Oxford.

MACCOBY, E. and C. JACKLIN (1974) The Psychology of Sex Differences. Palo Alto: Stanford University Press.

MAINARDI, P. (1970) "The politics of housework," pp. 447–454 in R. Morgan (ed.) Sisterhood is Powerful. New York: Vintage.

MALOS, E. (1980) The Politics of Housework. London: Allison and Busby.

MARKS, S. (1977) "Multiple roles and role strain: Some notes on human energy, time and commitment." American Sociological Review 42 (August): 921–936.

MASIH, K. (1967) "Career saliency and its relation to certain needs, interests, and job values." Personnel and Guidance Journal 45, 7: 653–658.

MEISSNER, M., E. HUMPHRIES, S. MEIS, and W. SCHEU (1975) "No exit for wives: Sexual division of labor and the cumulation of household demands." Review of

Canadian Sociology and Anthropology 12 (September): 424–439.

MODEL, S. (1981) "Housework by husbands: Determinants and implications." Journal of Family Issues 2, 2: 225–237.

MORGAN, C. (1980) "Female and male attitudes toward life: Implications for theories of mental health." Sex Roles 6, 3: 367–380.

MORGAN, J. (1978) "A potpourri of new data gathered from interviews with husbands and wives," in G. Duncan and J. Morgan (eds.) Five Thousand American Families— Patterns of Economic Progress, vol. 6. Ann Arbor, MI: Institute for Social Research.

MORGAN, R. (1970) Sisterhood is Powerful. New York: Vintage.

MYRDAL, A. (1967) "Introduction," in E. Dahlstrom and R. Liljestrom (eds.) The Changing Roles of Men and Women. London: Duckworth.

———and V. KLEIN (1956) Women's Two Roles: Home and Work. London: Routledge.

NEWSON, J. and E. NEWSON (1965) Patterns of Infant Care in an Urban Community. Harmondsworth, UK: Penguin.

NICKOLS, S. (1976) "Work and housework: Family roles in productive activity." Paper presented at the National Council on Family Relations, New York.

———and E. METZEN (1982) "Impact of wife's employment upon husbands' housework." Journal of Family Issues 3, 2: 199–216.

NOLAN, F. (1963) "Rural employment and husbands and wives," pp. 241–250 in F.I. Nye and L.W. Hoffman (eds.) The Employed Mother in America. Chicago: Rand McNally.

OAKLEY, A. (1974) The Sociology of Housework. New York: Pantheon.

ORZACK, K. (1959) "Work as a 'central life interest' of professionals." Social Problems 7, 1: 73–84.

OWEN, M., L. CHASE-LANSDALE, and M.E. LAMB (1981) "Mothers' and fathers' attitudes, maternal employment, and the security of infant-parent attachment." Unpublished paper, University of Michigan.

PARSONS, T. and R.F. BALES (1955) Family Socialization and Interaction Process. Glencoe, IL: Free Press.

PEARLIN, L. (1975) "Sex roles and depression," pp. 191–207 in N. Datan (ed.) Life-Span Developmental Psychology: Normative Life Crises. New York: Academic Press.

PERRUCCI, C., H. POTTER, and D. RHOADS (1978) "Determinants of male family role performance." Psychology of Women Quarterly 3 (Fall): 53–66.

PIOTROWSKI, J. (1971) "The employment of married women and the changing sex roles in Poland," pp. 73–90 in A. Michel (ed.) Family Issues of Employed Women in Europe and America. Leiden: E.J. Brill.

PLECK, J.H. (1977) "The work-family role system." Social Problems 24 (April): 417–427.

———(1978) "Males' traditional attitudes toward women: Conceptual issues in research," pp. 617–644 in J. Sherman and F. Denmark (eds.) The Psychology of Women: New Directions in Research. New York: Psychological Dimensions.

———(1979) "Men's family work: Three perspectives and some new data." Family Coordinator 24 (October): 94–101.

———(1980) "The work-family problem: Overloading the system," pp. 239–254 in B. Forisha and B. Goldman (eds.) Outsiders on the Inside: Women in Organizations. Englewood Cliffs, NJ: Prentice-Hall.

———(1982) Husbands' and Wives' Paid Work, Family Work, and Adjustment. Wellesley, MA: Wellesley College Center for Research on Women.

——— (1983) "Husbands' paid work and family roles: Current research issues," pp. 251–333 in H. Lopata and J.H. Pleck (eds.) Research in the Interweave of Social Roles, vol. 3: Families and Jobs. Greenwich, CT: JAI Press.

——— and L. LANG (1978) Men's Family Role: Its Nature and Consequences. Wellesley, MA: Wellesley College Center for Research on Women.

——— and M. RUSTAD (1980a) Husbands' and Wives' Time in Family Work and Paid Work in the 1975–76 Study of Time Use. Wellesley, MA: Wellesley College Center for Research on Women.

——— (1980b) Methodological Issues in Analyzing Paid Work and Family Work in the 1975–76 Study of Time Use. Wellesley, MA: Wellesley College Center for Research on Women.

POGREBIN, L. (1983) Family Politics: Love and Power on an Intimate Frontier. New York: McGraw-Hill.

POLATNICK, M. (1973–74) "Why men don't rear children: A power analysis." Berkeley Journal of Sociology 18 (Winter): 45–86.

PRESSER, H.B. (1977) "Female employment and the division of labor within the home: A longitudinal perspective." Paper presented at the Population Association of America, St. Louis.

QUINN, R.P. and STAINES, G.L. (1979) The 1977 Quality of Employment Survey. Ann Arbor, MI: Institute for Social Research.

RADLOFF, L. (1975) "Sex differences in depression: The effects of occupation and marital status." Sex Roles 1 (September): 249–265.

RICE, R., J. NEAR, and R. HUNT (1980) "The job-satisfaction/life-satisfaction relationship: A review of empirical research." Basic and Applied Social Psychology 1, 1:37–64.

ROBERTS, M. and WORTZEL, L. (1979) "Husbands who prepare dinner: A test of competing theories of marital role allocations." Unpublished paper, Boston University.

ROBINSON, J.P. (1977a) How Americans Use Time: A Socio-Psychological Analysis. New York: Praeger.

——— (1977b) Changes in Americans' Use of Time: 1965–75 -- A Progress Report. Cleveland, OH: Communications Research Center, Cleveland State University.

——— (1977c) How Americans Used Time in 1965. Ann Arbor, MI: Institute for Social Research.

——— (1980) "Housework technology and household work," pp. 53–68 in S.F. Berk (ed.) Women and Household Labor. Beverly Hills, CA: Sage.

———, J. YERBY, M. FEIWEGER, and N. SOMERICK (1977) "Sex-role differences in time use." Sex Roles 3 (October): 443–458.

ROSENBERG, M. (1957) Occupations and Values. New York: Free Press.

RUSSELL, G. (1982) "Maternal employment status and fathers' involvement in child care." Australian and New Zealand Journal of Sociology 12: 28–35.

SAFILIOS-ROTHSCHILD, C. (1970) "The influence of the wife's degree of work commitment upon some aspects of family organization and dynamics." Journal of Marriage and the Family 32, 4: 681–691.

——— (1972) "Companionate marriage and sexual inequality: Are they compatible?," pp. 63–73 in C. Safilios-Rothschild (ed.) Toward a Sociology of Women. Lexington, MA: Xerox College Publishing.

SANIK, M. (1979) "A twofold comparison of time spent in household work in two-parent, two-child households: Urban New York State in 1967–68 and 1977." Dissertations Abstracts International 39 (April): 5334B.

———(1981) "Division of household work: A decade comparison — 1967–1977." Home Economics Research Journal 10, 2: 175–180.

———(1983) "Differences in workloads of husbands and wives." Unpublished paper, Ohio State University.

SCANZONI, J. (1970) Opportunity and the Family. New York: Free Press.

———(1975) Sex Roles, Life Styles, and Childbearing: Changing Patterns in Marriage and the Family. New York: Free Press.

———(1978) Sex Roles, Women's Work, and Marital Conflict. Lexington, MA: Lexington Books.

———and SZINOVACZ, M. (1980) Family Decision-Making: A Developmental Model. Beverly Hills, CA: Sage.

SCHAFER, R. and P. KEITH (1980) "Equity and depression among married couples." Social Psychology Quarterly 43 (4): 430–435.

SCHRAM, R. (1984) "Moms, supermoms." New York Times Book Review, Sept. 16, 1984, p. 9.

SCOTT, D. and B. WISHY (1982) America's Families: A Documentary History. New York: Harper and Row.

SEARS, P. and A. BARBEE (1978) "Career and life satisfactions among Terman's gifted women," pp. 28–65 in J. Stanley, W. George, and C. Solano (eds.) The Gifted and the Creative: Fifty-Year Perspective. Baltimore: Johns Hopkins.

SEARS, R. (1977) "Sources of life satisfaction of the Terman gifted men." American Psychologist 32, 2: 119–128.

SELIGMAN, M. (1974) "Depression and learned helplessness," pp. 218–239 in R. Friedman and L. Katz (eds.) The Psychology of Depression: Contemporary Theory and Research. Washington, DC: Winston.

SIEBER, S. (1954) "Toward a theory of role accumulation." American Sociological Review 39 (August): 567–578.

SLOCUM, W. and F.I. NYE (1976) "Provider and housekeeper roles," pp. 81–100 in F.I. Nye (ed.) Role Structure and Analysis for the Family. Beverly Hills, CA: Sage.

SMITH, R. (1979) "The movement of women into the labor force," pp. 1–30 in R. Smith (ed.) The Subtle Revolution: Women at Work. Washington, DC: Urban Institute.

SPENCE, J., R. HELMREICH, and J. STAPP (1974) "The Personal Attributes Questionnaire: A measure of sex role stereotypes and masculinity-femininity." JSAS Catalog of Selected Documents in Psychology 4:43.

STAFFORD, F. and G. DUNCAN (1978) "Market hours, real hours, and labor productivity." Economic Outlook USA (Autumn): 103–119.

STAFFORD, R., E. BACKMAN, and P. DiBONA (1977) "The division of labor among cohabiting and married couples." Journal of Marriage and the Family 39 (February): 43–57.

STAINES, G.L. and J.H. PLECK (1983) The Impact of Work Schedules on the Family. Ann Arbor, MI: Institute for Social Research.

———J.H. PLECK, L. SHEPARD, and P. O'CONNOR (1978) "Wives' employment status and marital adjustment: Yet another look." Psychology of Women Quarterly 1978 (Fall): 90–120.

STEWART, A. (1978) "Role combination and psychological health in women." Paper presented at the Eastern Psychological Association.

STUEVE, A., L. O'DONNELL, and L. LEIN (1980) "What Should Daughters Do?": Framing Commitments to Elderly Parents. Wellesley, MA: Wellesley College Center for Research on Women.

SZALAI, A. (ed.) (1972) The Use of Time: Daily Activities of Urban and Suburban

Populations in Twelve Countries. The Hague: Mouton.

VANEK, J. (1973) Keeping Busy: Time Spent in Housework, United States, 1920–1970. Doctoral dissertation, Dept. of Sociology, University of Michigan.

——— (1974) "Time spent in housework." Scientific American 231 (May): 116–120.

——— (1980) "Household work, wage work, and sexual equality," pp. 275–292 in S.F. Berk (ed.) Women and Household Labor. Beverly Hills, CA: Sage.

VERBRUGGE, L. (1982) "Women's social roles and health," pp. 49–78 in P. Berman and E. Ramey (eds.) Women: A Developmental Perspective. Washington, DC: National Institutes of Health.

VEROFF, J., E. DOUVAN, and R. KULKA (1981) The Inner American. New York: Basic.

VICKERY, C. (1979) "Women's economic contribution to the family," pp. 159–200 in R.E. Smith (ed.) The Subtle Revolution: Women at Work. Washington: Urban Institute.

WALKER, K. and W. GAUGER (1973) "Time and its dollar value in household work." Family Economics Review (Fall): 8–13.

——— and M. WOODS (1976) Time Use: A Measure of Household Production of Goods and Services. Washington, DC: American Home Economics Association.

WRIGHT, J. (1978) "Are working women really more satisifed?" Journal of Marriage and the Family 40 (May): 301:314.

YANKELOVICH, D. (1974) The New Morality: A Profile of American Youth in the 70's. New York: McGraw-Hill.

YOUNG, M. and P. WILLMOTT (1973) The Symmetrical Family. New York: Pantheon.

About the Author

JOSEPH H. PLECK is Associate Director of the Wellesley College Center for Research on Women, and is Director of the Center's Male Role Program. His major publications are *Men and Masculinity* (1974), *The American Man* (1980), *The Myth of Masculinity* (1981), *The Impact of Work Schedules on the Family* (1983), and *Families and Jobs* (1983). Pleck was previously affiliated with the Center for the Family at the University of Massachusetts at Amherst, and the Institute for Survey Research at the University of Michigan. He holds a Ph.D. in clinical psychology from Harvard University.